D0699363

POINT LOMA COLLEGE LIBRARY
3900 Lomaland Drive
San Diego, CA 92106

Call Number

Accession Number

150.7
B863d

129677

Broadbent
IN DEFENCE OF EMPIIRICAL PSYCHOLOGY

In Defence of
Empirical Psychology

BY THE SAME AUTHOR

Perception and Communication (1958)
Behaviour (1961)
Decision and Stress (1971)

150.7
B863d

In Defence of
Empirical Psychology

Donald E. Broadbent F.R.S.

POINT LOMA COLLEGE
129677
RYAN LIBRARY

METHUEN & CO LTD

First published in Great Britain 1973
by Methuen & Co Ltd
11 New Fetter Lane, London EC4

© *1973 Donald E. Broadbent*

Printed in Great Britain by
The Camelot Press Ltd, London
and Southampton

SBN 416 76780 X

Distributed in the USA by
HARPER & ROW PUBLISHERS, INC.
BARNES & NOBLE IMPORT DIVISION

TO MARGARET
who worked and didn't talk

Contents

FOREWORD   *page* ix

*Part 1   Uncertainty and Action: The William James
          Lectures 1971*

1 Introduction: The Definition of an Action   3
2 Choice, Probability and Perception   21
3 The Combination of Evidence   40
4 The Use of Emotional Words   65
5 The Recall of Particular Memories   82
6 Optimal Strategies of Mental Organization   103

Part 2   Some Particular Issues

Perceptual Defence and the Engineering Psychologist 123
The Well Ordered Mind   143
Aspects of Human Decision-Making   163
In Defence of Empirical Psychology   187

Postscript   208

REFERENCES   210

INDEX   219

Foreword

If one is engaged in research and application in a rapidly moving field, one tends to get submerged in technical detail. During the last few years that has certainly been true of me; but at intervals I have been invited to talk to relatively non-specialist audiences, and have had to pause briefly on each occasion to take stock. Each time the pause has got longer, because I have gradually come to realize that technical psychology is getting stranger and stranger to those in other disciplines; and each speciality in psychology is getting stranger to the others. Furthermore, assumptions which can be taken for granted between those brought up in the same place and time need to be spelled out for those of different background or age. Unless this is done, extraordinary misinterpretations arise, and psychologists may be criticized for holding views which are in fact quite foreign to them. This seems a pity, since no doubt there are plenty of mistakes in the views they do hold: and effort might better be directed at these.

As an attempt at bridge-building, therefore, I thought it might be worth while to gather these talks together. In each case I have kept the oratorical rather than the abstract scientific style: and left the phrasing as it was devised for the original audience. The policy is deliberate, because I hope these lectures will convey the way in which psychological research grows out of particular people in particular contexts. Thanks to the sociological devices of modern science, it nevertheless achieves some communication across gulfs of educational and temperamental difference. That is why I believe in it.

Part I

UNCERTAINTY
AND ACTION

The first six lectures were given as the William James Lectures at Harvard in the spring of 1971. They give a very general and sketchy account of one man's view of the state and role of the experimental psychology of human beings at that time.

1 Introduction
The Definition of an Action

On the 28th day of April 1958, a Viscount airliner belonging to British European Airways was approaching the airport at Prestwick in Scotland. The pilot called up Prestwick on the radio, announced that he was at 14,500 feet, and requested permission to descend in order to land. The airport gave him permission, and he commenced descent. He called again at 12,500 feet, and again at 10,500 feet. Shortly after the last call, the airliner struck the ground. The subsequent enquiry established that the pilot had misread the indications on his instruments, and that the aircraft had always been 10,000 feet lower than the pilot thought.

The traditional approach to an event of this kind could be phrased something like this. The commander of an aircraft is a person, who therefore is responsible for his actions. He has an experience of the outside world, and is endowed with reason which will calculate for him the likely consequences of each of his acts. He also has certain desires and preferences, and in the light of these he makes a choice. In addition to the immediate obvious consequences of that choice, there may also be legal retribution for actions which are thought to be socially undesirable: which may help to counterbalance some of the private selfish desires which might otherwise sway a person too far.

This traditional description contains a good deal of value. Nevertheless, there has during this century grown up the view that the traditional description needs to be altered and amplified in important ways, to bring out rather different features of the human condition. The accident to Viscount G–AORC provides an interesting example of this second approach. Viscounts of that date were equipped with a three-pointer altimeter: and this in itself will explain the accident to any engineering psychologist such as myself. For those who come from different backgrounds, I should explain that an altimeter of this type consists of a clock face numbered from zero to nine, and carrying three pointers of different lengths. The longest pointer indicates the height in hundreds of feet, the next longest the height in thousands of feet, and the shortest the height in units of 10,000 feet. Since each pointer moves steadily round the scale, the smallest pointer will be nearly at one when the next largest pointer reaches nine. That should properly be interpreted as meaning an altitude of 9,000 feet: but it can very easily be read as 19,000. In many other situations in life, we are used to reading a pointer to the nearest digit, and it is hard to break this habit in this particular case. In addition, the task is made particularly difficult by the relative length of the pointers, which associates the largest errors with the smallest and least visible point (see Rolfe 1969).

These criticisms of the instrument have been backed by laboratory experiments on the ease with which it can be read, and also by surveys of accidents. It seems inescapable that such accidents were sometimes due, not to a negligent choice by a person placing his own slothful ease above his responsibility to the community, but rather to the combined characteristics of the instrument in front of him and his own perceptual apparatus. Just as it has long been held in the courts that failure of reason may lessen human responsibility, so equally it seems fair to hold that a failure of perception may do the same. In general, this approach to human nature prefers to probe deeper into the traditional concepts of person, reason, perception, or choice; and to analyse these terms into a complex of inter-related parts, which form an intelligible (although exceedingly complicated) system. Each part in the system must be logically connected with an observable event, which principle has recently been stated by Jerry Fodor as the central feature of 'behaviourism'. I shall therefore use that name as a quick way of referring to my own attitude, without of course necessarily wishing to support any other views which may be ascribed to behaviourists by their enemies* (Fodor 1968).

Why now do I start this series of Lectures with this very elementary problem of an aircraft instrument? Traditionally, the posture of the experimental psychologist has been to show a low profile. He concerns himself with tiny details of the learning of nonsense syllables, of the refinement of psychophysical methods, of the meaning to be attached to statistical tests using one-tail rather than two-tails of the distribution. His approach is pre-eminently that of the so-called 'silent generation' which returned to Universities from World War II, and which in contrast to their fathers or their sons, raised no protests, went on no marches, and issued no manifestoes. It is therefore often assumed that the views of the silent generation are the same as those of the silent majority, and it is usually further assumed that both groups are traditionalist and conservative. This is by no means a necessary assumption, and it may be quite a dangerous one at a time when the silent generation is beginning to reach positions of influence and authority throughout the world. Nevertheless, the assumption is often made: and it does at least fit in with the concern of the experimental psychologist for detail, his apparent lack of interest in ideology, and his reluctance to talk about broader issues.

I myself belong to this profession and this generation, and I fully share its values. Accordingly, I will promise my professional colleagues that there will be something for them in these Lectures: there will indeed be tachistoscopes, measurements of reaction time, human beings on line to computers, and free recall of long lists of words. In particular, I think I can promise that every Lecture

---

* Fodor of course rejects behaviourism in this sense; briefly, I hold that his arguments against it always involve some extra postulate (e.g. that the observable event should occur on the same occasion as the internal event connected with it). I therefore regard his arguments as insufficient.

will contain at least one previously unpublished experiment. Having thus established some degree of respectability, however, I want also to relate what I say about experiments to certain broader issues. I have two main reasons for doing so.

First, I believe I am right in saying that this is the first occasion on which a psychologist from Cambridge, England, has given these Lectures in Cambridge, Massachusetts. It follows that I have to be aware of possible errors and ambiguities in communication between one culture and another. Of course, it is hardly accidental that both our cities share the same name, and this provides the common basis which makes it worth while to get some message across. All the same, I cannot administer to you stimuli which will produce standard reactions in my own society, and expect confidently to get the same response from you. Neither can you use, in assessing my attitudes, the same rules as you employ with an American. Sometimes, the basic information is simply not available. For example, when sitting on the other side of the Atlantic awaiting eagerly my weekly ration of culture, in the shape of *Newsweek*, I learn that Americans may infer something about the political attitudes and beliefs of their colleagues by observing the presence or absence of a bumper sticker or lapel badge carrying the Stars and Stripes. I will present you freely with the information that my bumper does not bear such a sticker: but it is trivial that you can draw no legitimate inference from this whatever. For all you know I might quite well be exactly the kind of person most likely, if I were an American, to carry such a sticker.

Another difficulty is that familiar symbols change their meaning: and that highly charged issues become irrelevant. This can be very dangerous ground, and I shall only venture gently on to it just far enough to show what I mean; and then withdraw hastily. As my first example, I will present you again with the information that I display prominently on the wall of my office a reproduction of the U.S. Declaration of Independence. But the meaning of this may not be quite the same as it would in America. I recall that some years ago a Socialist Foreign Secretary from my

6

country suggested to the then President that, although American policy might quite well be justified, nevertheless 'a decent respect for the opinions of mankind' might recommend a rather more open style in explaining it. As I understand it, this comment gave great offence, since it was not felt that the words of Thomas Jefferson should be bandied about by foreigners.

That illustrates that a traditional symbol in one culture becomes quite the reverse in another; but what about relevance? Let me take a typical political issue from my country, which aroused strong feelings. In the spring of 1971 there was a proposal, which I thought quite wrong and to be resisted, to return in Northern Ireland to a very dangerous practice. I mean the practice of policemen going about their normal business carrying guns. To Americans such an issue could scarcely seem one of primary importance. Even in the U.K. by the autumn of 1971 and following a major change in the use of violence in Ulster, the issue had become utterly academic; and on balance and with regret, my own views had reversed. Now, think of the political issue which concerns you most; and realize that to me that question probably seems as remote and secondary as the question of arming policemen does to you. Relevance is culturally determined, and specific to a time and place.

Because of these cultural differences, I cannot take for granted that you share my basic orientation; that the test of intellectual excellence of a psychological theory, as well as its moral justification, lies in its application to concrete practical situations. Quite apart from the personal problem of a British speaker to a largely American audience, however, there is a further reason for surrounding technical discussion of psychological topics by general examination of the reasons for my methods and the implications of my results. In the United Kingdom there is at this time a wave of questioning or doubt concerning the traditional approach of experimental psychology. Thus we find Dr Joynson of Nottingham (Joynson 1970) writing a paper whose very title is 'The Breakdown of Modern Psychology'. We find Professor Hudson of Edinburgh remarking that some of his students feel that behavioural psychology is 'part of a capitalist plot designed to prevent students from asking searching questions, not merely about the nature of their own disciplines, but about the roots of power in the society in which they find themselves' (Hudson 1970). Recent publications by Dr Ingleby of the London School of Economics (Ingleby 1970), and by Dr Shotter (1970) in the *Bulletin of the British Psychological Society*, might also be quoted in criticism of the traditional behaviouristic style of psychology.

This mood of criticism may be purely British, but I do not think so. In the U.S.A. one notices George Miller feels it desirable to spend most of a Presidential Address to the A.P.A. talking about the broader place of psychology (Miller 1969). American visitors to our own shores in recent months have confirmed that a similar questioning of empiricism is at work amongst you also. Donald Schon, giving the Reith Lectures on the B.B.C., points out devastatingly that factual information on the size of the immigration problem to New York city could not be collected until it was too late for it to be used, and that many similar facts make an empirical approach to political action impossible (Schon 1971). He prefers an 'existential' approach, a significant adjective. Professor Moynihan of Harvard, talking to our Social Science Research Council, has recently argued that social scientists are falling out of favour with progressive political thinkers in the States, because they normally advise that nothing can be done quickly, which is of course seen as meaning that nothing ever will be done (Moynihan 1970). Professor Chomsky speaking in my Cambridge has commented adversely on the relative amounts of information collected by empirical scientists concerning society in Thailand, and concerning the role of the Standard Oil Company in American Government (Chomsky 1971). Last but not least, John W. Campbell, the late and much lamented editor of Analog science fiction, has recently attacked psychology, as being unscientific since it cannot produce reconciliation and communication between two people who approach a problem from different attitudes.*

---

* In an editorial during the winter of 1970–1. Alas, the Cambridge reference libraries do not stock Analog and my copy is lost.

My own position is, as you might guess, that I think this criticism mistaken. If I may select one of these distinguished names as an opponent, I think I would choose the editor of Analog, and reply that the failure of psychologists to produce reconciliation of personal differences is matched by the failure of physicists to produce anti-gravity machines, and still more drives to make space ships travel faster than light. I will allow physics this failure, however, because such problems are very difficult, and there is really quite tolerable success in describing the fall of apples, and other problems of that kind. Correspondingly, psychologists are pretty good at three-pointer altimeters. But here I unmask my concealed batteries, because the experimental work which raised serious question about the altimeter was done more than ten years before the Viscount accident with which I started this Lecture. A further seven years went by before the United Kingdom Altimeter Committee recommended an alternative instrument, and as of 1970 there is still no legislation to prohibit continued use of multi-pointer displays. Accidents of this kind are still occurring.

There are a number of reasons for the delay of nearly a quarter of a century in stopping these unnecessary accidents. From personal involvement in the battle, however, I am quite sure that a substantial cause of the resistance has been in the continued presence of the traditional philosophical attitude which I described earlier. So far from viewing an experimental and behaviouristic analysis of the human system as a tool of existing society, I think that it is flatly contradictory to many features of that society, but nevertheless is insidiously changing society in ways which I approve. From my point of view, the critics of a behaviouristic and experimentally oriented approach to human beings represent the last kicks of an outdated culture, which has had great value in its time, but which has now outlived its usefulness. Nevertheless, only a barbarian would wish to lose the achievements of our traditional civilization, and it is important to understand the sound judgments and values which underlie the mistaken criticism of behaviourism, even though I think that criticism mistaken.

During the past fifty years, such criticism has traversed three philosophical areas. First. there were the problems associated with the relationship of purpose and mechanism. Next. there were the problems of mind and matter. But in my view, the common thread in the recent critics I have mentioned lies in their concern with the concept of control. If we analyse human nature scientifically into a system made up of intelligible and causally related components, this must surely expose the individual man to manipulation by those who know the correct stimuli to apply to him. This concern shows itself perhaps most clearly in Chomsky's argument; but equally it appears in the discussions by Ingleby or by R. D. Laing of the danger that psychiatrists may control the patient whom they purport to be helping. Such a control by one person of another would seem morally wrong to many people brought up in the traditional Anglo-Saxon culture: the widespread concern expressed about subliminal advertising is an example of this distaste. In addition, however, there is a strong intuition in many people that such control would in fact be impossible, and that the nature of human beings is not such as to permit it. On this rather different ground therefore any approach which is seen as aiming at control or manipulation is also open to criticism as factually wrong. The objection to the concept of control is therefore two-fold: it cannot be done, and in so far as it can be done, it should not.

The objection to my own school of thought, therefore, is based essentially on the kind of philosophical problems which have in the past been discussed under labels such as Freedom and Determinism. The massive attention given to problems of freedom by Jean Paul Sartre, whose thinking is closely associated with some of the critics of behaviourism, is by no means coincidental. These problems are not purely academic and intellectual. It is clear from the immediate appeal of Sartre to many living in our society that the problem of freedom is one which people nowadays feel to be a close and personal concern. Now I too would share the distaste for the concept of control which I have just tried to state; although it seems to me merely a counsel of despair to return to traditional concepts of mind. I regard it as a fair criticism of the behaviouristically inclined that we have not taken account of moral dangers in, or intuitive inadequacies of, our approach. I felt therefore that, in these Lectures, I would try to weave together a number of themes at different levels; not merely to state some experimental facts and generalizations, but also to use them as illustrations of broader issues. I hope that the specific experiments may interest my professional colleagues: I am quite sure that those colleagues will support my broader attitudes, because these are very traditional. Fearlessly and without thought of consequence I shall declare myself against sin; openly and with vigour I shall be in favour of motherhood. All the same, if a lot of people are saying that motherhood is a servile state imposed on reluctant women by chauvinistic males, and if others are suggesting that sin is a label given to behaviour calculated to disrupt bourgeois enjoyment of the property exploited from the workers, it may be worth spelling out what different meanings may be attached to those terms. By weaving together themes on different levels, I expose myself rather seriously to the danger of attempting too much and falling flat on my face. All the same, it is possible my prostrate body might be used as a stepping stone for other people to reach for higher things.

At the scientific level, therefore, I want to make three points in these Lectures. First, our nervous system is limited both in size and in reliability: with the result that much of its functioning is designed to take account of these limitations. Large areas of mental life can only be understood once this point is grasped.

Secondly, I want to urge the importance in human behaviour of the theorem generally associated with Bayes. As is widely familiar, that theorem states that confidence in a particular hypothesis is closely connected with our confidence in alternative hypotheses: and in particular, when we get some relevant evidence, to the ratio of the probability of the evidence given the hypothesis on one hand and its alternative on the other. There is now quite a lot of evidence that our involuntary behaviour obeys this theorem, at least in approximate form, and I would urge that our voluntary behaviour ought also to conform to it.

Thirdly, I want to emphasize the importance of optional rather than obligatory strategies in mental performances. There is an unfortunate habit of mind amongst most researchers: they look for a constant rule of behaviour which will apply to all people, and to the same person on all occasions. Much recent work however shows that quite different strategies of performance can be adopted regularly by different people, or from time to time by the same person.

These three points are already quite broad at a scientific level, but in addition I shall have two further themes which are even broader, and transcend the particular subject of psychology. The first of these more general themes is that my view of experimental psychology forms part of an integrated attitude to science as a whole and to life in general. I have a vision of what is going on in the twentieth century, which is doubtless as inadequate as any other, but into which my view of psychology does at least fit consistently. My second general theme is the inadequacy of traditional mental concepts.

So much for preliminaries, and on to some facts. Even the rest of this Lecture, however, will differ from later ones in containing less new experiments and fewer novel ideas. This is because, to get to the novel areas, I need to start by considering why the problems of purpose and mechanism no longer worry us very much. Amongst our predecessors in the time of J. B. Watson, men of goodwill were seriously concerned about that problem: the mechanisms they knew, such as clocks or motor cars, were such as to repeat identical sequences of actions always in the same way. They were therefore worried by an attempt to analyse behaviour in scientific terms, because it seemed to leave out of account the purposive quality of action. Was not purpose a category of explanation quite different from the causality involved in clockwork?

Let us take an example of a human action. Being who I am, I think naturally of the act of drinking a cup of tea. My hand moves out, contacts the handle of the cup, raises it to my lips, and tips the contents down my throat. But only in a very general and abstract sense can it be said that my picking up of a teacup today is the same as the operation which took place yesterday. Examination of the muscular contractions and detailed movements would show that they were quite different each time. To make observation easy, let us concentrate on one part of the process, the movement of my hand to the teacup. In order to get the measurements out into observable form, let us furthermore replace the motion of my hand, which is difficult to instrument satisfactorily, by the motion of some object under my control, which has got to be brought to a satisfactory coincidence with some target points.

I can now introduce an experimental facility which was for some years an ornament of our lab in Cambridge, and which was used by my colleague, Dr Hammerton. Outside our building, there is a large and attractive English garden; and across the back of the house there ran a small model railway. On this railway there was a trolley, which could run along the track; and at the side of the track were small target markers which lay concealed behind the track until the experimenter wanted them, but which when he chose could rise suddenly into a visible position standing at the side of the track.

The experimental subject was at the far end of the garden, and therefore as he looked in the direction of the laboratory, he saw the trolley move across his field of view. In one hand he held a small control, by moving which he could vary the speed of the trolley; so what he had to do was to watch for the target marker appearing somewhere in his range of vision, and then to move the trolley as fast as possible to line it up with the marker.

One cannot conceal the fact that this experiment was great fun. The end which we had in view, however, was a practical and highly expensive one. The training of pilots or car drivers is dangerous and costs money, because they have to operate in the actual vehicles which they are subsequently going to control. Simulators have been devised in both cases, in which the man can go through the actual movements which he will need to use in a car or plane. If only one could do all the teaching in such simulators, we could save a lot of money and a lot of potential danger. But unfortunately it is always found that the man being trained does require quite a lot of time in the air or on the road, and no simulator has yet given perfect training without such real experience. Equally, however, any simulator can be accused of being slightly different from the real thing. When one tells a simulator designer that the training is imperfect, his natural reaction is therefore to ask for another million dollars to build a slightly improved simulator.

Dr Hammerton therefore reversed the usual line of attack; by building his model railway or Toy Train, he was constructing a real system which we could simulate perfectly rather than approximately. We could take our experimental subject to the end of the garden, leave him the small control which he held in his hand, and conceal from him the motion of the real train. In front of him we could instead put a small screen, on which was projected a spot of light whose position was controlled by the position of the train on the real track; which he was in fact really controlling. Thus the motion of the spot on the screen corresponded exactly to the motion of the train on the track. Every other feature of the situation, such as the chair he sat in, the nature of the control, or even the singing of the birds, was exactly the same.

A man doing a task of this sort improves with practice, and he does so at about the same rate whether he is practising on the simulator or with vision of the real track. You might think that all he has to do is to learn to make two movements, of appropriate size and with an appropriate time interval between them. The first movement is to apply a velocity to the trolley which sends it towards the target: and the second is to remove that velocity so that the trolley stops exactly at the target. As we shall see, this is very much an oversimplification, but the point we need for the moment is merely that whatever the sequence of movements involved, it should be the same in the simulator and in the real thing. The crucial test is to transfer a man from the simulator to the real task, by training him on the simulator and then removing the screen so that he can see the real track. I am afraid that on the first trial after this change, his performance goes right back to the original level as if he had no training whatever (Hammerton 1963a).

If one looks at the situation more analytically, one can see the reasons for this. First, the actual movements of the man do not repeat themselves, and they are far more numerous than the logical minimum. Unpublished work by Tickner and Poulton in which the actual number of movements was recorded and counted shows that there are two or three times as many as the ideal minimum in a task of this kind. Secondly, the behaviour falls into two successive stages. Although the movements in each stage may be different, we can always distinguish the two, and they always follow each other. Furthermore, each of them is affected in different ways by particular features of the task.

In the first stage, the trolley is a long way from the target and has to be brought close to it. A limit here is the maximum speed of the trolley. The second stage, however, is the final settling of the trolley exactly in line with the target, and here the maximum possible velocity is unimportant. The difficulty is rather that tiny or accidental jerks on the control must not send the trolley hurtling off and away from the target. The man does badly in this second stage therefore if there is a high 'gain' of the system, that is, if the velocity of the trolley changes a lot from a small control movement. These two factors work together in a complicated way which can create havoc if you are trying to decide on the best value of gain to build into the system. There will be such an optimum (a) *if* changes in gain vary the maximum system output (trolley velocity in our example) (b) *if* the target and trolley need to be very precisely aligned, so that the settling stage is really difficult. Neither of these conditions need apply, and Hammerton has shown experimentally that when either condition fails to be met, there is no sharp optimum value of gain (Hammerton 1962, 1964a).

Furthermore, with the Toy Train one can ask the man to perform the task at various distances from the track. This alters the gain, defined as rate of change of visual angle for unit control movement. Yet a man can do the task just as well at long range or at short range, and does so even if his vision is restricted, so that his perceptual constancy is abolished and he is thus prevented from perceiving the true tather than the angular velocity of the trolley. The reason for this lack of effect of range is that performance is limited by maximum trolley velocity, which does not alter at different ranges (Hammerton 1963b).

For our purposes, the main point is that this simple action consists of two segments, each of which is defined by its final state, and not by the movements which take place. The detailed movements in the first segment can be any of a large class, and those in the second segment any of another class. Any member of the first class can be combined with any member of the second class. If we go back to my drinking a cup of tea, we see that the same is true: the segments of approaching my hand to the cup, moving the cup to my mouth, and tipping the cup, may each be performed in many different ways, even though the three segments normally follow each other.

This property of behaviour, of consisting of a series of segments each of which may contain any member of a large class, is an extremely general one. It is by no means uniquely human: if you watch a monkey catching nuts thrown to it at the zoo, you will see it catch each nut with a completely different movement, and then bring it to its mouth with a movement once again different on any occasion. Only the sequence of the two segments remains constant. Similarly, consider the long and elaborate forms of behaviour characterized as instinctive. As our grandfathers were fond of pointing out, the hunting wasp will paralyse its prey, drag it to the nest, lay eggs within it, and seal up the nest before departure. Yet the stinging of the prey is never accomplished by the same movement on two different occasions, nor is the approach to the nest, nor any other stage of the behaviour. If one describes each stage by some abstract label, then the sequence of these abstract descriptions remains constant; yet at the surface level of direct observation no instinctive action is the same as any other. Finally, think of the simple two-word sentences of children, in which any member of one class of words may occur in the first position, and any member of another class in the second position: Daddy gone, Johnny hot; Johnny gone, Daddy hot, and so on. Once again the number of such sentences may be very large if we observe them at the level of words, but they are all identical if we describe them as a sequence of two classes described abstractly.

This last illustration leads on to the general properties of language, which have aroused a great deal of interest lately. If I say the sentence 'A large pink rabbit stood behind the boring lecturer', it is likely that you will recognize this sentence as grammatical even though you have never heard this particular sequence of words previously. If, however, one describes each segment of the sentence abstractly, and examines the sequence of abstract descriptions, then this sentence is the same as that which describes 'The quick brown fox jumped over the lazy dog', and a large variety of other grammatical sentences. Linguists have been rightly fascinated by this property of language, producing unique sequences which nevertheless obey general rules. This property, however, is by no means unique to language, nor indeed to human beings, but rather is a property of most behaviour down to that of insects. The unusual features of language should be sought elsewhere: for example, in the degree of environmental support which each segment of the behaviour gets.

As I warned you, most of what I have been saying is familiar territory for psychologists. To take an analysis of a decade ago, Miller, Galanter and Pribram (1960) proposed a terminology for the analysis of behaviour into structures which they called 'plans'. Each plan consisted of a sequence of segments, each segment being defined by the goal which it was trying to achieve.

The goal was set up by switching on a functional element, a TOTE unit, inside the organism: and this unit remained in control of behaviour until its appropriate goal was achieved. Apart from one very interesting suggestion, which I shall come to in a moment, Miller, Galanter and Pribram left open for later study the detailed way in which a TOTE unit could actually produce appropriate movements; of course, completely random behaviour would in the end secure the goal, but that is a rather rare and in-efficient system. There are a number of other possibilities, of which we can distinguish three. As a matter of terminology, let us call the signal which sets up a goal, a 'command signal' for that goal.

First, the occurrence of a command signal might give rise to a sequence of lower-order command signals. For example, if I wish to go to Cambridge, England, I might say that this general goal can be achieved by going to Boston, then to London, and then to Cambridge. This leaves open the question of whether I go to Boston by bus, subway, or taxi, whether I go Boston–London by sea or by air, or by which airline, and whether I travel London–Cambridge by train, bus, or car. I can in fact use any combination of methods, so that if I did the journey every day of my life (which God forbid) I probably need never repeat myself exactly. Further, I need not know when I start that I shall indeed find a way of making the last step: the last train may have gone and the taxis all vanished. This technique is therefore heuristic rather than guaranteed to succeed. It is the one put forward by Miller, Galanter and Pribram, and it will result in the formation of a hierarchy of segments of behaviour, each level including the lower one. The lowest level of all might be one of random move-ments, but only that. This technique of setting sub-goals is also embodied in computer programs for solving logical problems, such as the programs of Newell, Shaw and Simon (1958) or Newell and Simon (1972).

A second possibility for producing detailed movement is that a command signal may set in motion an established closed loop control system, in which the size and direction of the discrepancy between the command and the state of the world is used to launch some movement which is known to reduce the discrepancy. The effect of this movement in turn will be detected and give another movement, and so on. The familiar mechanical analogy is a domestic heating system where a thermostat turns on the heating if the room is too cold, and turns it off when the termperature rises enough.

A third possibility is that the command signal may set off a sequence of pre-programmed movements, which have repeatedly been appropriate in getting the desired effect. Here we are back to clockwork or the starting of a car. Although each of these possibilities has had its advocates in psychology, it is likely that all of them exist in human behaviour. Dr Hammerton's work again is relevant.

Imagine a screen with a spot of light, and a control lever moving in two dimensions. One could mount the lever beneath the screen so that the hand is placed on it by extending the arm towards the screen: and one can connect the lever to the spot by making a movement upwards send the spot up, and a movement to the right send the spot to the right. Alternatively, one could swing the lever and the arm round at right angles to the line of sight to the display. In this position, the same muscular movements which send the spot upwards mean that the lever is pushed at right angles to the spot movement: the lever goes west when the spot goes north. Untrained men placed in this situation do much worse than they do in the one I first described. Apparently they work on a spatial rule, and try to move the lever in the same direction they want the spot to go. Once practised in the easy situation, however, they can then opperate the difficult one immediately – their muscles do the right thing straight away, and they have apparently shifted the task from a series of spatial goals to an automatic series of movements (Hammerton and Tickner 1964b).

Animal examples can also be cited. At relatively low levels of practice, a rat learns a spatial arrangement rather than a detailed motor pattern: if he is taught that food lies east of an intersection which he has approached from the north, he will turn right (a new movement) when he is made to approach the intersection from the south. But an animal highly practised on a very routine motor pattern will be less flexible: if he is taught to run down a runway and turn into an opening halfway down, an unexpected shortening of the runway will cause him to pass the opening and bang his head hard against the wall shortly after it (Carr and Watson 1908).

19

It is likely then that each of the suggested methods of organization does actually appear in behaviour. All of them have common characteristics. First, they are sound modern engineering practice for the design of a complex system with unreliable components and a varying environment. It is dangerous for any such system to work like the old Prussian army with orders prescribing everything that is to done. Rather, one should use command signals which are executed locally in ways which will vary with local and temporary conditions. Secondly, each of these methods is started by a command signal. This is the core of our contemporary answer to the problems which our fathers had over purpose and mechanism: human action is not like clockwork, but nevertheless the purpose of an action is a state of the man which precedes that action. It does not require some mysterious causality by states of the world which are still in the future. So far as any one man was responsible for our modern satisfaction on this point, I would say that it was Clark Hull of Yale: but in any event the issue is now dead, and nothing I have said is particularly original or novel. I apologize for this: but I needed to establish as a basis for further advance that the key point in voluntary action is the occurrence of a command signal. As William James (1890) so graphically described it, an anticipatory image of the sensorial consequences of a movement, plus (on certain occasions) the fiat that these consequences shall become actual, is the only psychic state which introspection lets us discern as the forerunner of our voluntary acts. In the next Lecture, I shall consider the various mathematical models which one might derive from William James's introspections, and compare them with the results of experiment to see how well our wills do really conform to his brilliant intuitions.

2 Choice, Probability and Perception

At the end of the previous Lecture, we had established that a human action is defined by a command signal which initiates it, and which corresponds to the state of affairs which will complete it. An action is not defined as a particular sequence of movements or anything of that sort. We recalled also that William James, in his introspective analyses, rightly placed emphasis on the occurrence of an image of the desired goal as an essential factor in voluntary action: but I said that his account still had certain inadequacies. Let me take an instance which has recently been cited by Professor Audley of London (Audley 1970). James describes himself lying in bed before getting up in the morning. He lies there until there occurs to him the idea of himself out of bed, without any of the concomitant discomforts of cold, exertion, and so on. One could interpret this description in a number of ways: perhaps the most obvious is to suppose that there is a series of events inside William James, of which one corresponds to the command signal which interests us, and the others do not. We could then suppose that the signal of interest will occur with a particular probability, and that the sequence of events will proceed, until such time as the desired signal does in fact occur. The question then is whether the probability of the appropriate command signal remains constant throughout the process, or whether it changes as time goes on: the mentalistic or introspective language is unclear on this point, and one might conceivably interpret James as supposing that no event was of relevance until the idea of the action came into being.

This, however, is false to fact. One can see how it may be tested by considering two alternative actions rather than only one. Let us suppose that William James usually got out of the right hand side of his bed, but occasionally out of the left hand side: perhaps he aimed at getting out of the right side on working days and the left side at weekends, or something of that sort. Until one of the two command signals occurred, he would lie in bed. Then the probability that there will be a delay of t units of time, followed by William James getting out of the right side of the bed is equal to the probability of inaction for one instant raised to the power t and multiplied by the probability of the appropriate command signal. Equally, the probability of getting out of the other side of bed is equal to the probability of inaction raised to the power t and multiplied by the probability of the other command signal. Now it happens to be the case that these two expressions imply that the average time taken to decide on the probable action will be the same as the average time taken to decide on the improbable one.*

We now have a logical relationship between the events supposed to go on in William James's mind, and quantities which are observable, such as the probability of an action and the time taken to decide to make it. We can arrange a suitable situation in which a man is choosing between pressing one of a number of keys, and in which he is more likely to press one key than another. We can then measure how long he takes over each decision: and it has been found in a large number of experiments that he takes much longer to press the unlikely key than he does to decide to press a probable one.

We can therefore rule out the idea that the probability of choice of an action remains constant throughout the time leading up to the decision. We have to suppose that something is going on inside the man which causes the chance of a decision in favour of a particular action to get higher or lower, so that we must speak of him during his process of decision as being nearer one choice at

---

* For more formal discussions of this and the arguments which follow on decision times, see Broadbent (1971) Chapter VI, Laming (1968), Audley and Pike (1965).

one time than he was at a time a little previously. At each instant there must be an increment in the chance of one decision, or a decrement, or perhaps no change at all. The final outcome must be some kind of total of the events over a series of instants. There are a lot of different ways in which this could be done in detail, but there are certain broad classes of theory which we can distinguish experimentally, and it is quite profitable to do so.

First of all, let us make the point that it is very reasonable for the mechanism of choice to be of this general kind. One of the ways in which our brains differ from computers is that the components are highly unreliable: a nerve cell does not fire with the consistency of a relay or an electronic switch, but rather with a probability that depends upon all kinds of factors of temporary state. If human action depended only upon an instantaneous event, then our decisions would have only the reliability of a judgment about the relative merits of the climate in England and Massachusetts obtained by looking at the incidence of rain on one day. Yet the average of a large series of events is a stable and reliable quantity: if we count how many days in the year have rain in England and Massachusetts, it is likely that we shall get a reliable result, even though there may be quite a lot of individual days on which it was raining in America and not in England.

But what kind of average or other rule should one adopt in arriving at a decision? Let us take this question of deciding which country is the wettest, and think of some examples. One might take observations on a series of days, and say that the first country to reach some specified critical number of wet days would be regarded as the wettest. A second possibility is that we might take the difference in the number of wet days on the two sides, and wait until that difference had reached some critical value. You can see these two approaches are rather different, because one of them might give a decision in favour of England even if it had rained almost as much in Boston that year: it is really a method which decides whether England is wet, and not a method which considers the *balance* of evidence between two hypotheses. There are other possibilities as well: but the other possible methods can be arranged between these two extremes. At one extreme, there are methods which resemble the running of a race, in which the winner is the first to reach some critical level. At the opposite extreme, there are methods which rather resemble a different kind of race, in which the winner is the first to establish a lead of greater than a fixed amount.

If we think then of a human voluntary action, it becomes sensible to enquire which of these broad methods approximates to the system which we ourselves employ. If the launching of the action is preceded by a series of successive events, some of which are impulses in favour of one choice and some of another, are these combined by a rule which considers only the first alternative to reach some necessary total of impulses, or is it rather a matter of the size of the discrepancy between different alternatives? To distinguish these possibilities can be done, but it means looking more closely at the sources of the stream of impulses which lead up to the voluntary act.

In order to understand this, let us examine a little more closely how the two classes of theory would explain the fact that the more probable action takes place faster. For brevity, let us call the theory of 'first past the post wins' the Horse Race Theory. It is harder to find a name for the other theory, in which the winner is the first action to gain a lead of a certain extent. Let us call it the Tennis Theory, because in tennis one must win by at least two points. The name is imperfect, because a game of tennis can be won by *more* than two points, but it will serve. Now the Horse Race Theory predicts quite directly that probable actions will take place faster. If at any instant the probability of an impulse in favour of one action is greater than the probability of an impulse in favour of another, then on average any critical number of impulses in favour of the more probable action will be built up more rapidly. The Tennis Theory needs some slight modification, because even if an impulse to one action is more probable than an impulse in favour of another, yet the average time taken to build up a critical difference between the total number of impulses will be the same regardless of whether the difference happens to come out in favour of the more probable action, or of the less probable action. However, this does not mean that we can rule out the Tennis Theory straight away, because there is an element in the theory which can be manipulated so as to produce the right result: that element is the critical difference between actions which are necessary before the winner is declared. If the more probable action requires a smaller lead to win, then it will in fact occur faster as well as more frequently. This might quite well be a sensible mechanism, under certain circumstances.

Suppose we go back to the question of assessing the relative amounts of rain in Cambridge, England, and Cambridge, Massachusetts. Instead of asking which was wetter in general, suppose we make an investigation for each month of the year separately. We might well find that most of the months showed more rain in England, but that there were, say, two months in the year when there were more wet days in Massachusetts. A decision in favour of England as the wettest would then be more probable, simply because there are more months in which that is true and fewer months in which the opposite is true. However, in the minority months it might well be that the probability of a wet day in Massachusetts was higher, and of a wet day in England lower, than was true in the rest of the year. If now we used the Horse Race method in making our decision, we should find for the two abnormal months that decisions in favour of Massachusetts as the wettest were faster and those in favour of England slower, even though throughout the rest of the year decisions in favour of England were faster and those in favour of Massachusetts slower. This is because the Horse Race Theory goes on the probability of an individual wet day. Suppose we adopted the Tennis Theory, however, with the modification I mentioned earlier. That is, suppose that we would require a smaller lead in wet days for England than we would for Massachusetts. In that case, decisions in favour of England would come out faster whether they were in the two exceptional months, or in the rest of the year.

I am afraid this is a bit confusing: the trouble is that we have

25

129677

got two senses in which probability is being used, which are a bit different. There is the probability-regardless-of-what-month-it-is that England is wettest, and there is the probability-in-this-particular-month that you will have a wet day in England rather than Massachusetts. Let us try and simplify things by distinguishing 'correct' decisions from 'errors', and say that for ten months of the year the correct decision would be England, and any decision for Massachusetts would be an error; but for the remaining two months the correct decision would be Massachusetts and England would be an error. Then on the Horse Race Theory correct decisions are always faster than errors, while in the Tennis Theory decisions in favour of England are always faster than decisions in favour of America. Other things being equal, the Tennis Theory would say that it will take as long to decide that England is the wettest when that decision is correct, as when that decision is an error.

Now we can turn to an experiment on human beings. If for instance we give a man two reaction keys and two lamps, and also on each trial light up one of his lamps, we may quite well invite him to press the key which corresponds to the particular lamp that has been lit. If one lamp lights more often than the other, then it is more probable that one key will be pressed than the other. Nevertheless, there will be correct decisions and errors both to the probable light and to the improbable one. We can then ask the question whether the correct key is faster than the errors, or whether the more probable key is always faster regardless of its correctness.

Such experiments have been conducted by many people, and broadly speaking I would declare the result to be in favour of the Tennis Theory, and not the Horse Race Theory. That is, the same reaction usually takes the same length of time whether it is made correctly or in error. What this suggests is that the fiat of the will does not occur simply when one tendency reaches a critical point, but rather when the balance between the action and its alternatives becomes sufficiently uneven. We have therefore made two points: (1) actions are chosen by some gradual cumulative process; (2) that process is a balance between alternatives. I now want to argue (3) there is more than one process.

There are several lines of evidence on this. First of all, although it is broadly true that an error reaction takes the same time as the same reaction made correctly, yet there are some kinds of experiment in which the error times are slightly *faster* than the correct ones. Although this is not in accordance with the Tennis Theory, it is in the wrong direction for the Horse Race Theory, and therefore gives no aid or comfort to that point of view. Dr Rabbitt of Oxford has recently clarified the basis of the discrepancy very considerably. As you will know, most of us are included in a number of computer data banks for credit cards, social security records, etc. It is a regrettable feature of the process of punching data into computers that the probability of an error in digital material is somewhere around 1 in a 1,000, which with the number of entries being made annually in any civilized country represents a fair number of cases of individual turmoil. An important question is whether the computer operator can recognize that a given key punch was in error and immediately press some other key to cancel the previous stroke. The answer is that they can, quite frequently, do so. From a practical point of view, this means that one should provide such a key. But there is also a theoretical interest in the result: one can consider separately the speed with which the operator made these errors which can subsequently be corrected, and the speed with which other errors were made of which the person making them remained unaware. It is found that the former are especially fast reactions, and that the latter take the same length of time as correct reactions do.

Thus it seems that one has to consider two successive stages in the process of decision. There are a certain number of actions in which the command signal that issues in movement differs from some other signal, which is held elsewhere inside the man. This other signal is available for comparison with the action that actually occurs. Greatly daring, let me call this earlier signal the 'intention'. Now we seem to need two processes of averaging or cumulation, the first producing a stable intention from some earlier unreliable activity. The second process then converts the intention into an action. The second process may sometimes have too risky a criterion, and thus produce an unintentional error. When, however, enough time is allowed to make sure that the action is in accordance with intention, yet nevertheless the intention itself may be wrong. In that case at least one stage of the process must act on the Tennis Theory, because right and wrong actions take the same time; although it is not certain that both stages must.

The same conclusion, that there are two distinct processes rather than one, is supported by another line of evidence. Although one gets evidence in favour of the Tennis Theory from most experiments on reaction time using clearly distinct signals such as the lighting of lamps in different places, there is another kind of experiment which gives rather different results. Suppose we ask a man to discriminate lines of two different lengths, where the discrimination is quite difficult. In such a case, certain experiments do seem to show that errors may be slower than the corresponding correct responses. On the face of it, this would be evidence for the Horse Race Theory. In so far as the other experiments reject that theory, we would have to suppose two mechanisms present rather than one. One might suppose that the choice of a command signal is performed by some process working on the Tennis principle, but that there is also some mechanism which only becomes important if a man is trying to distinguish two very similar states of the outside world, and this mechanism perhaps might work on the Horse Race principle. Certainly one can see that the distinction of a line from another line of very similar length would create problems for an unreliable system such as the brain, and that evidence would have to be accumulated just as we have supposed it to be in the choice of a particular action. Because of these experiments also, therefore, it seems reasonable to think of two successive processes, of which the first accumulates evidence from the outside world until it has become sufficiently clear what the situation is. The output from this first mechanism is then fed to a second mechanism, in combination with the desires and preferences of the man, until a second average or accumulation over time has taken place, whereupon an action is launched.

There is a good deal of other evidence about the necessity of supposing two successive stages. Thus for example it has long been known that simple reaction time to sound will be slightly faster when the stimulus is intense rather than faint. Once one has got the idea that action takes place when enough evidence has accumulated, one can see that an intense stimulus would provide evidence more rapidly and therefore reach any particular criterion sooner. But consider the case of two sounds which have equal intensity, and yet differ in duration. Perhaps one of them lasts only 40 msecs, while the other lasts 70 or 80. It has been shown by Tony Sanford in Cambridge, England, that the reaction time to the long sound is faster than that to the short one. This is apparently paradoxical at first sight because it means that the reaction occurs quicker if there is stimulus energy present later on in time as well as earlier. However, the longer duration sound not only gives a faster reaction, but also sounds louder. The apparent paradox disappears if one supposes that the sound is averaged or integrated at a first stage, and that a signal representing the total loudness is then averaged or integrated again until a critical level is reached to produce reaction. Sanford has also shown that, if one presents a sound while a man is watching a clock, the effect of making the sound louder is to make it appear at an earlier time on the clock, so far as the subject reports. It is then actually perceived earlier. The size of this effect on the time of perception, however, is smaller than the effect on the time of key-pressing: and it seems therefore that a more intense stimulus speeds up, not only the perception of an event, but also the process of launching the action which follows on that event (Sanford 1969, 1971).

Let us get a little less abstract and link this idea of two successive processes in decision to a practical situation. I have noticed upon one occasion in the traffic surrounding a certain North American city, an affluent gentleman driving and simultaneously talking on the telephone. This is certainly a technological possibility, but one wonders whether it is altogether wise. In some studies undertaken for the British authorities on this subject, Dr Brown asked his victims to drive a car towards a narrow gap, while answering messages heard over a loudspeaker. Their task was to decide whether or not the gap was sufficiently wide to drive through: and if they thought it possible, to carry on and do so. Various sizes of gap were used, and the changes in behaviour with and without the telephone messages were noted. The perception of a telephone message can perhaps fairly be regarded as an early stage in the cascading process I have mentioned earlier. Correspondingly, it did not seem to interfere with the ability of a man to drive through narrow gaps: for any given size of gap, he made no more errors in driving than he did without the telephone message. What did happen, however, was that the reception of a sound message made it more likely that he would attempt to get through a gap which in fact he would not have been able to pass even under normal conditions. So the early stage of deciding to try or not try was subject to interference from another perceptual task: but the execution of the decision, once taken, was perfectly unaffected (Brown, Tickner and Simmonds 1969). Similar tendencies for interferences to occur between two decisions, but not between a decision in one task and the execution of a decision in another have been found in another experiment on car driving in England: and also in an important series of studies by Trumbo and Noble in the United States (Brown, Simmonds and Tickner 1967; Trumbo and Noble 1670).

We have to think then of the selection of a command signal, the fiat of the will, as the result of at least two processes which have the general character of an average or accumulation of a variable series of events, and where the result of the first process is used as an input to the second process. There may actually be more than two stages, but no matter how parsimonious we are I think we must assume at least two. One of these processes has to work on the Tennis Theory: the other might work on the Horse Race Theory, although actually I do not think we are compelled to believe that it does. But there is at some point a setting of criterion to correspond with probability, which is in fact highly rational because it minimizes the number of errors.

Let us go earlier in the process, and see how similar principles apply in the perceptual part of the system. I have already said that the brain is made of unreliable components, so that it is very unlikely that any particular impulses in any particular nerve cells will occur predictably and consistently whenever a particular stimulus strikes our senses. In addition, we are being bombarded all the time by a very large quantity of information: and in relation to this large quantity of information we are all, like Winnie the Pooh, bears of very little brain. Any machine for recognizing patterns makes use of a lot of components, and it is likely that the analysis of all possible patterns of stimulation amongst those falling on the senses would stretch our available machinery to the limit. How then could we make use of the fact that some things in the world around us are more likely to happen than others are? Broadly, there are two possibilities. The first is that we might look specifically for things which are more likely to happen, so that we get more evidence about them. For example, if we are meeting a stranger at an airport, we might supply ourselves with a photograph or a description, and compare each person coming through the gate with the photograph to check whether or not they have the features of the desired person. A similar process might take place inside the brain, through the bringing into action of recognition mechanisms for particular features which are likely to occur in certain circumstances. In terms of an accumulation of evidence by a Horse Race or a Tennis Theory, the actual evidence will be more reliable about a probable event. There is the other possibility, however, that the perceptual process also, like the one which decides on action, may set a slacker level of evidence for a probable event than it would for an improbable one.

This is, perhaps, the point to stand back from the particular field of psychology and think about scientific method in general. There are three broad strategies which people put forward as the best line of attack in science, that is, as the best way of attaining knowledge about the nature of the world. Interestingly enough, each of these theories of scientific method has associated with it a corresponding theory of individual human perception. That is, each belief about the way one ought to study physics or bio-chemistry has a corresponding theory about the way in which the brain actually detects the presence of a table. Let us consider the theories of scientific method first, and then the perceptual theories later.

The first approach might be termed pure positivism. On this doctrine, the scientist wanders through the world observing at random, and the facts of nature inexorably compel him towards certain generalizations and inductions. This view is not now popular, and it is rather hard to find anybody who really believes in it.

Much more fashionable is the second view, which one can call the hypothetico-deductive approach. On this view, the scientist should set up a theory, predict the consequences from it, and make observations selectively about the truth or falsehood of the predictions. If the predictions are true, he may continue to hold his theory; if they are false, he has to change it. Proponents of this view point out rightly that most scientists do not observe at random, but that the process of discovery is normally guided by an idea: and they are also fond of pointing out that you can never prove a theory, but only disprove it. I should say that this view was probably the dominant one in most areas of psychology.

However, it can itself be criticized fairly severely by exponents of the third view. This third attitude I would call Bayesian, and the essence of it is that, when one investigates a problem, one should not only consider one pet theory, but also consider what alternatives there may be. Proponents of this view criticize hypo-thetico-deductive method on the grounds that psychologists at least very often test their pet theory by predicting from it a fact which is also predicted by a very large number of other theories. This, so a Bayesian would say, is not terribly productive: further-more, if one does predict a fact which turns out to be false, unless one has formulated some alternative hypothesis one is left very badly at sea. The temptation is to ignore or explain away the awkward fact. The proper course is to divide the array of possible theories into an exhaustive set of classes, and then to make observations whose result is very improbable on some classes of theory, and very probable on others. The relationship to which one is appealing is Bayes' Theorem, which in the form I want to use is best expressed by saying that if there is a hypothesis *H*, and an observed state of the world *S*, then after observing *S*, the odds on *H* are equal to the odds before *S* was observed multiplied by the ratio of the probability of *S* given *H* to the probability of *S* given not *H*.

$$\frac{P_S}{1 - P_S} = \frac{P_N}{1 - P_N} \times \frac{P_C}{P_F}$$

P_S = probability of theory given a datum *S*
P_N = probability of theory before the datum
P_C = probability of *S* given theory correct
P_F = probability of *S* given theory false

The usual objection to Bayes' Theorem is of course that it may be true mathematically, but it is exceedingly difficult to apply in practice, because we may have no information about some of the factors involved.

Now let us think of corresponding theories of perception. First of all, there is the theory that perception is purely passive. On this view, we are stimulated by the outside world, and the events at our senses cause a corresponding state of the brain. This theory of perception is like positivism in science, and it is just about as unfashionable and unpopular. The snag is that there are all kinds of effects on perception from properties of the man himself: you see what you expect to see, or what is probable. A man may confidently experience some event which certainly did not happen: and it is clear that a perceptual experience may or may not occur for reasons which have nothing to do with the nature of the outside world but only of the man who is perceiving.

The second theory of perception, then, is the active theory, which corresponds to the hypothetico-deductive approach in science. On the active theory, a man approaches the world with a hypothesis about the event he is likely to meet: he has a kind of model inside him of the most probable state of the world, and he tests this model against the information coming from his senses. If it turns out false, he may discard it and put up another model, but as long as nothing disproves it, he will maintain it. As in the case of scientific method, this active theory of perception is probably the most fashionable at the present day. You can see that it has no difficulty whatever in explaining that people will see probable events more easily than improbable ones, and that the various factors which make a man more ready to try out one perception rather than another will greatly affect the chances of his having one experience or another.

I myself support a third theory of perception, which corresponds to the Bayesian approach in scientific method. You might call it a 'Biassed Passive' theory of perception; the essence of it is that you get evidence from your senses about what is going on in the world, but that it takes far more evidence to convince you that something unusual is happening than that something perfectly normal is going on. Instead of trying out just one possible model of the world, you have a whole array of other possible models, and the evidence of your senses decides between these rather than merely confirming or disproving one. I support this kind of view by doing experiments on the perception of words, by finding (as everybody does) that it is easier to perceive words which are common in the language, and also that the misperceptions which are produced are more usually common words rather than uncommon words. On assumptions which seem to me plausible and which involve the Tennis Theory, I can calculate that the greater tendency to produce a common word as an error is exactly sufficient to account for the greater tendency to produce a common word as a correct perception (Broadbent 1967). But as this line of experiment is quite old, let me talk about some new work which points to a similar conclusion.

If you hold an active theory of perception, you suppose that the brain interrogates the outside world to find out whether or not certain features are present: if one is thinking of the perception of written words, for example, it might be quite plausible that feature recognition systems which would detect the presence or absence of certain common features in words might be put into readiness. Mechanical devices for character recognition will examine a visual pattern for the presence of straight lines in particular orientations, curves that are concave downwards, and so on: and it would be rational to test first for probable features, and only later for improbable ones. We do not know what visual features human perception might use, but if we think of written words it is likely that common features will be contained in common letters of the alphabet. So if we simply took words from the language, words which contained common letters of the alphabet might well be more detectable than words which do not: and it is known that common words are in fact more likely to contain common letters. So perhaps on the active theory we might perceive common words better because they contain common letters. For various reasons it is hard to check this using words drawn from everyday English, although I have had a go at it (Broadbent and Gregory 1968). It is much less objectionable, however, to take a small fixed vocabulary of words, which the subject knows, to present these words to him in very brief flashes, and to use some of the words more frequently than others within the experiment. Now if one uses the set of words 'bad, pat, bat, pad', one can manipulate the probability in various interesting ways. For example, by presenting BAD and PAT each on 40 per cent of the trials, and the other two words equally often on the remaining trials, one obtains words which are unequally probable but made up of letters which are equally probable. If on the other hand one presents BAD on only 4 per cent of trials, and the other three words equally often on the remaining trials, then one has three words of equal probability which differ in the probability of their letters. So one can distinguish the three theories of perception by looking at the results in these two conditions: the pure passive theory, which nobody believes, would simply say

35

that there would be no effect of probability. The active theory, at least of the type which contends that one looks for probable features of the stimulus, would predict that the first experiment would show no difference between the words, but in the second experiment there would be a difference between the three equally probable words. Lastly, the biassed passive theory would expect difference between the words in the first experiment, but no difference in the second since the three words are equally probable. In fact, the results are those one would expect from the biassed passive theory (Broadbent and Gregory 1971).

There is a quite different line of attack which brings us to the same conclusion. Suppose one asks a man to listen over a noisy telephone line to the sounds PAH and BAH, which differ only in the phonetic feature known as voicing. A level of performance can then be measured, and it will be greater than the number of correct perceptions found if the listener is presented with a larger array of sounds PAH, BAH, TAH, DAH, which differ both in voicing and in the place of articulation. On an active theory of perception one might well argue that the need to analyse two phonetic features rather than one would explain the drop in the number of correct perceptions: because it would be harder for the active process to match two sets of features rather than one. However, suppose we score the performance in a rather different way. When the sound PAH has been presented, if the man reports it as TAH he is in fact correct so far as the absence of voicing is concerned, even although he has got the place of articulation wrong. Similarly, if the sound BAH was presented, then DAH is correct as far as voicing is concerned. Dr Clive Holloway has measured the efficiency with which each phonetic feature is perceived in large vocabularies and in small ones, and finds that there is no effect on the efficiency of detection of each individual feature when one is listening to a large vocabulary of sounds rather than a small one. The drop in probability of completely correct perception is merely caused by the fact that a larger number of features increases the probability that at least one feature will be misperceived. There is no evidence of selective tuning of the perceptual system to one feature when it is certain that feature will be relevant to perception (Holloway 1970).

These kind of experiments, as well as a number of others and ones being reported in the next Lecture, make me fairly confident that the active theory of perception is false. When we perceive more efficiently some event which is probable, that is not because we set up a hypothesis that this event is about to occur, and test selectively for the stimulus features which it would possess if it were indeed there. Rather, we take in evidence from our senses (admittedly distorted and incomplete) about whatever the true event may be: and when we have summed and combined this evidence, we demand a smaller weight of evidence to produce a perception of a probable event than of an improbable one. The effect of probability is through a bias on a decision process, and not through selective intake of information related to certain features.

Now, let me summarize. When a man decides on an action, we know that the process of choice must have been some kind of accumulation or totalling of evidence over time, and also that this process must have been based on a conflict or decision between various alternative actions, rather than simply acting on a sufficiently strong impulse even when others are pretty strong. There seem in addition to be at least two successive processes of averaging or totalling, the result of the one being fed into the input of the next.

This kind of averaging process is sensible, because on a priori grounds one would expect our brains to be rather unreliable at any given moment: and in fact we know empirically that men sometimes perceive incorrectly, and that sometimes even when they have perceived correctly their action disagrees with their intentions and is in error. Although therefore there seems to be an unreliability in the system, the critical levels which the averaging process needs to reach are adjusted so that the total number of correct outcomes is higher than would be possible for the same rate of working without an adjustment of the criteria. We have got here an example of the adaptation of the brain to

37

its own limits of capacity and reliability, which I mentioned in the first Lecture as being one of my themes. At present it may seem a little abstract, but I shall be going further into this process in the next Lecture. I am heading for the gross distortions of perception which take place in social situations, and which I think can be shown to stem from the relatively rational adjustment of the brain to its own limitations.

One of my other themes, the role of Bayesian processes, has also been touched upon although not very emphatically as yet. You will have noticed, however, that I believe our normal process of decision decides between alternatives rather than accepting the first action of sufficient strength, and furthermore that our perception of the world is not based upon testing the truth of a single hypothesis, but rather collecting evidence to decide between a very large number of possibilities. You will have noted the relationship to scientific method: and I hope particularly noticed that I did not set up a single theory of the process of choice to test its predictions. Rather, I tried to set out exhaustively the various kinds of theory that could exist, and to decide broadly which classes were acceptable and which not. On the whole, however, this has not been a Lecture with very much application outside psychology. May I finish by pointing out the wider relevance of some of the concepts?

I sometimes toy with the idea that belief in the various theories of perception might be associated with belief in the corresponding theories of scientific method, and also of politics. Just possibly, all believers in pure positivism might also support the passive theory of perception, and also support a political theory in which control by the environment was dominant. Just possibly, belief in a single strong political ideology might encourage a belief in rationalism rather than empiricism in science, and in the active organization of perception by the man himself. I myself believe in the third possible approach in all three fields, including politics. To some extent, my political approach has been institutionalized in various countries, one of the recent examples being the growth since World War II in Britain of a system whereby each officer of government has another person in the opposition party who deals with the same branch of affairs and whose function is to form every possible different diagnosis from the minister in power. Such a system has been called (by your Vice-President amongst others) the 'adversary system': I think quite wrongly. I think the term is unfortunate, because the whole point of the system is not that Prime Minister Smith should defeat and ignore Opposition Leader Jones, but that Smith should take serious note of the arguments advanced by Jones, and act on them when faced with an event which is hard to fit into his own categories. Perhaps at this point I should act according to my own principles, and say that there is doubtless a good deal to be said against this speculation. Yet, if I want to recommend to you my own approach to politics and to science, perhaps the first step is to consider how efficient our brains are, using such a system in perception, and that will be the main topic of the next Lecture.

3   The Combination
of Evidence

In the previous two Lectures we have defined human action as the setting up of a goal or command signal which will in turn produce detailed movements and operations to achieve the goal; and we have seen that selection of a command signal results from an accumulation or averaging process, deciding between alternatives, while fed with information about the state of the world. We noticed that both in perception and in action, the system adjusts itself to overcome its own unreliability, and the inadequacy of its evidence, by altering the criteria in the averaging or accumulation process. But I was talking in the previous Lecture as if action was based only on the perception of one event; and this is a very rare situation. Much more usually, we have available several sources of information or items of evidence, and these must in some way be combined before they give rise to action. Social situations provide quite interesting examples of the process. Suppose, for example, that in some emergency, such as the landing of an aircraft unexpectedly in a small town where there is a shortage of accommodation, you have to choose between sharing a room for the night with one of two people. One person might be a dry goods salesman from Iowa, a member of his local Rotary and secretary of the P.T.A. The other is a male ballet dancer from Greenwich Village who is a subscriber to the *New York Review of Books*. I do not think you will have much difficulty in combining these items of information to decide which is the man for you.

The curious nature of this process is well illustrated by taking somebody from another culture, such as myself. Of course some of the predictor information about my likely behaviour in various circumstances is already available to you. Some of you may even think that the likely mentality of a white Anglo-Saxon Protestant is almost too familiar to you. One can go further: for example, by saying that I am not only a Protestant but also an Episcopalian. This indicator also will give you a distinctly better than chance probability of predicting any of my attitudes. For example, a recent Canadian study shows that my religious group is less likely than any other to attribute deviant behaviour to moral wickedness, but rather to 'sickness'. Even Jews and those of no religion apparently have a greater tendency to the high moral line than those of my persuasion do (Shaw 1970). As one gets further away from American culture, your awareness of the significance of different group memberships may get rather weaker: if I say that I was at Winchester, Cambridge, and in the Royal Air Force, this may carry something of the same flavour as of an American who says that he was at Groton, Yale, and in the U.S. Air Force, but not quite. Beyond this point we get into failures of communication, and also into a realm where new items may shed quite a different light on the picture one has drawn thus far. For example, although I am heavily anglicized, I am in fact Welsh rather than English; and this will in Britain modify and alter general expectations of my likely responses. To give you the flavour quickly, in my judgment it is more probable in Wales than in England that your bank manager will write poetry in his spare time, and it is more likely that he will have a cousin who is a coal miner. If you have been trying to predict my attitudes from the previous information I have given, that ought to add a note of doubt, which I could strengthen by adding the information that my family income was *not* what you might rashly have inferred from hearing that I went to 'prep school' (or public school, as we call it).

As group memberships are one of the more interesting predictor variables, it is worth while having a look at the nature of my old school rather more closely. The stereotype of that school in

Britain has quite a number of features, of which one need only go into one to give the flavour of prediction from group memberships. The school has been quite notable for two rather serious occupations by the boys, in which the staff were expelled from the buildings, the red flag hoisted, and preparations made to defend the premises against all comers. The Army had to be called out to restore order; these sad events are usually put down to the example of French happenings shortly previously. I ought perhaps to add at this point that I am not talking about 1968 and 1969, but about 1793 and 1817, the French example being an earlier French Revolution. However, the tradition still lives on: as you will be aware, my country has had Socialist governments in power for about half the period since World War II. In each such government there has been at least one ex-member of my school in a senior post, and usually more than one. More surprising even than this is the close family resemblance between the brand of Socialism advocated by each of these men. It has been in each case a highly unemotional and technical attack, which regards a sophisticated economic and social analysis as absolutely essential if any real progress is to be made. This kind of professionalism is part of the general culture of Winchester, even amongst those who are not Socialist politicians. The school provided, for example, both the Chief of Fighter Command in the Battle of Britain, and the Chief of Air Staff, Royal Air Force, for most of World War II. Nobody from this sub-culture is likely therefore to admire, shall we say, a leader of partisans who has a love affair and consequently blows the entire mission and is himself killed; you will doubtless realize whom I have in mind.

This kind of intellectualism, however, is not always popular. Professor Chomsky, when speaking recently in Cambridge, disagreed sharply with this brand of Socialism as expressed at the present time by Anthony Crosland (Chomsky 1971). Crosland was restating the view that Socialism is about the division of wealth and the allocation of resources; while Chomsky felt that this view was too narrow. He prefers Lord Russell's view of Socialism, as the liberation of the creative impulse. The danger of this view, as I see it, is that it can lead one to forget that a great many people are held back from feeling free and liberated primarily by the fact that they do not have any money. Alasdair Macintyre (1970) has recently criticized the views of Marcuse in a similar way, pointing out that they are very dangerous in so far as they distract from concern over welfare. To quote Macintyre 'The steady erosion of welfare institutions, the constant recreation of poverty is a part of the truth about modern industrial societies'. Peter Townsend recently argued in the London *Times* that the number of British children living below the poverty line is now three times what it was a decade ago. General vague talk about liberation is therefore not merely beside the point, but actively harmful, because it wastes time which ought to be spent in the production or analysis of specific suggestions for policies or institutions which might remedy this situation.

You will notice I have slipped from stating the stereotype which many people in Britain have of my school, to saying what I believe myself. Indeed, the value of knowing some of these group memberships of a person is that they do indeed predict, with a certain degree of unreliability, what his attitudes will be. For myself, one of my friends once summed me up by trying the game of locating the person in history whose post I would naturally fill, and he decided that the correct answer was 'Scientific Adviser to Oliver Cromwell'. I accept this characterization immediately, with both its good and bad parts. You will note that it agrees with some of the other predictor items I gave you earlier in attributing to me a combination of radicalism and traditional Puritan values, together with some overtones of scepticism about verbal doctrines in politics, and the need in the last resort to accept that most action will involve some unattractive elements. But beyond these similarities, the period of the early seventeenth century has always rather fascinated me, and as our own century has advanced it seems to me the resemblances between that period and this one have become more marked. They have been well set out by Sir Peter Medawar (1969): in the seventeenth century, most people were in doubt about questions of belief and authority, and their uncertainty and fumbling were expressed in repeated conflict and violence. The period lasted a relatively short time, however, ending with a new adjustment which in many ways has formed the basis of the advances of the intervening 300 years. The settlement had many sides to it, such as a shift in power from one kind of person to another within Britain: and also in a new attitude to the world which produced the founding of the Royal Society, and the beginning of a major phase in the exploitation by man of the physical world. I shall come back to this point in a later Lecture, because I suspect that in our own era a similar new settlement will indeed arise and bring a tolerably satisfactory solution to our present uncertainties.

More of that later: for the moment, the lesson of what I have been saying thus far is that we use information about each other, such as group membership, to predict attitudes and likely behaviour, and that although this information is unreliable it does do better than chance. Although there are a lot of things about me which you could not infer from my vita, the fact remains that I do share most of the opinions, attitudes, and values that somebody familiar with British culture would infer from looking at two or three lines of my history. Another point I shall come back to in a later Lecture is the meaning for human freedom of this determination by the group: for today, I am going to spend the rest of the time on considering ways in which information of different kinds combines.

There has been much work by social psychologists on person perception and related topics, ably summarized by Roger Brown (1965). Normally speaking, however, social psychologists use linear assumptions about the combination of evidence: experiments on individual people suggest different possibilities. I am going to talk about studies of an abstract laboratory kind.

First, there is the important point that getting information from one source does not appear to reduce the impact of another. This is sometimes described by saying that the effect of different channels of evidence is 'independent', although that word is rather ambiguous and needs to be specified very carefully (Garner and

Morton 1969). To demonstrate this principle of independence, let me consider a series of experiments by Dr Corcoran and his associates. In the first experiment, a man was asked to listen to a series of complex sounds. By 'complex' I mean that each sound had a number of different dimensions such as its pitch, the extent to which its intensity was going up and down, and so on. There was one particular sound which the man was trying to hear, rather like a husband listening for his wife's car coming home and distinguishing it from the cars of neighbours. So for each sound presented the man had to say whether it was the target sound or not.

If the sound presented resembled the target in every way but one, say pitch, then there was a certain probability that this difference would be detected. Let us call this probability P. Equally, if the sound presented resembled the target sound in every dimension except degree of amplitude variation, there was another probability Q that this difference would be detected. Then if one presented a sound which differed from the target in both the qualities rather than in only one of them, one can predict the probability R that this difference would be noticed by the equation

$$(1 - R) = (1 - P)(1 - Q).$$

That is, the man reports that the sound is a target only if he has failed to notice one dimension of difference *and* failed to notice the other dimension of difference. Furthermore, the chances of his failing on either dimension are the same as when he had only one dimension of difference available (Corcoran 1966).

This result is one which appears in a number of other situations. For example, Corcoran also studied the perception over a noisy telephone channel of the four words SAD SAT MAD MAT (Corcoran, Dorfman and Weening 1968). To bring out the resemblance to the previous situation, let us suppose that the probability of being correct on the initial consonant is P, and the probability of being correct on the final consonant is Q. Then the probability of being in error on both, and perceiving for example the word SAD when the word MAT was sent may be called $1 - R$, and once again

$$(1 - R) = (1 - P)(1 - Q).$$

These results are of course very similar to those obtained by Holloway or by myself, in the previous Lecture, and they show that when we are getting several different lines of evidence about some event, the actual evidence may come in just as effectively from each line whatever is happening on other lines. But thus far we have been talking about kinds of evidence which cannot possibly contradict each other, and merely fill out our knowledge of the event concerned. As an example from real life, consider the statements that I am British and also a psychologist: these give you information about two fairly different aspects of my likely behaviour, which are relatively unrelated. But one can also have cases in which the two lines of evidence may reinforce or contradict each other. The information that I went to a prep school, but had a relatively low family income, may create a conflict of judgment. There is a fairly long history of experimental work on such conflicts; it starts from a practical concern with the detection of contacts on sonar or radar screens. Possibly such detections might be better if the man was provided with information fed both to his eyes and also simultaneously to his ears. People do fail to see aircraft on radar screens, and one is always looking for ways of stopping this. If the explanation were simply to be that radar operators doze off, perhaps only for a second or two at a time, then of course the sleepy operator would fail to listen as well as fail to look. However, if the source of error lies in the fallibility and unreliability of our visual and auditory systems, then hopefully the errors introduced by intermittent failure inside our brains might be independent on the eye and on the ear. In that case, and if the operator reported a target with probability R whether he heard it, saw it, or both: then once again one might hope to find that

$$(1 - R) = (1 - P)(1 - Q).$$

This equation does in fact turn out to be approximately true, and this is quite a useful gain in performance of human operators (Buckner and McGrath 1963). But notice a rather odd assumption that has been built into the mathematics. If the man hears a target but does not see it, then his eyes are contradicting his ears: and similarly for the case where he sees the target but does not hear it. Yet we have assumed in each of these cases that the man acts according to the sense which is objectively correct. In a way, when his eye and ear were in conflict, it would surely be more reasonable to expect him to guess at random rather than to choose with some supernatural accuracy the sense which was in fact correct.

This is the point to remind you of Bayes' Theorem. The impact of some evidence upon the relative trust we have in two theories should be decided by the probability of that evidence given one theory and the probability of the evidence given the other theory. Now we hope, and experiment confirms, that our eyes and ears are less likely to report something which is not there than something which is there. Consequently if we receive the evidence that our eyes have detected something but the ears have not, it is in most situations rational to assume that the sense which is in error is the one which has failed to detect rather than the other one. This assumption may sometimes be wrong, but it is a sensible one. Corcoran has in fact provided evidence that behaviour lies between the two extremes: one does not guess at random when there is a contradiction between eye and ear, but neither does one decide always in favour of the objectively correct sense. The proportion of decisions which come out each way lies between the values that would be expected on each of these hypotheses, as if in cases of conflict one has a greater than chance tendency to choose the correct alternative (Corcoran and Weening 1969). In everyday practice, what this means is that when you can see something rather imperfectly and also hear it rather imperfectly, then you will in most cases do better to look and listen than to do either alone. Your failures of vision will not cancel out the advantage you gain from hearing, or vice versa. Two unreliable sources of evidence can be combined to give better performance than the average of the two.

Notice that the reason this is possible is because the evidence is considered, not merely in relation to one possible state of the world, but also to all the alternatives. One does not simply consider the probability that a signal will be heard and not seen; but also the probability that such a state of affairs will result from the *absence* of a signal. To take into account all the various alternative hypotheses, rather than just the probability of one, yields other ways of combining different sources of evidence so as to give a larger number of correct decisions than would be possible for

$$(1 - R) = (1 - P)(1 - Q).$$

For example, consider again the set of words MAD MAT SAD and SAT. Suppose that these were being read on a very poor carbon copy, so that perhaps M and S were completely indistinguishable, but T and D could be made out because of the distinctive shape of the D. Correspondingly, if the same words are heard rather than seen it might be that M and S could be heard perfectly, but T and D could not be distinguished. Now the probability of getting a word right by eye or ear alone may be 0·5, and yet the combination of the two sources of evidence may give 100 per cent correct performance. That is because the information that the word begins with M only raises the correct probability to 0·5, but it excludes completely the words SAD and SAT; and correspondingly the information that the word ends in D excludes completely SAT and MAT. Thus perfect performance can be obtained from two unreliable sources of information, provided that the whole range of states of the world is considered rather than merely one particular correct one.

The antithesis I am trying to suggest is rather like that of the previous Lecture, when I was talking about the speed of reaction, and distinguished the Horse Race Theory from the Tennis one. In the present Lecture, I am talking about the accuracy rather than the speed of performance; but once again I am contrasting an approach which concentrates only on the strongest alternative in play, and an approach that looks at all the alternatives. In the previous Lecture I talked about the gradual accumulation or summing of tendencies towards a perception or an action: today I am talking about the combination of impulses towards action derived from several sources. Just as in the previous Lecture, there are actually a number of different ways in which such a combination could take place, but it is useful to contrast two classes of theory. First, corresponding to the Horse Race model, there is the idea that one takes the strongest alternative indicated by each source, and combines those together. On the other hand, there is the idea that one looks at the impact of each source of evidence on *all* the alternatives in play, and takes the strongest resulting from this more complex process, which corresponds rather to the Tennis theory. One can distinguish these two broad classes of theory by strengthening or weakening the amount of evidence which is coming from one source, and then looking at the effect on behaviour.

You will remember that experiments by Corcoran, Holloway, and others showed that two sources of evidence act independently in the sense that

$$(1 - R) = (1 - P)(1 - Q).$$

By simple algebra, this implies that

$$R = P + (1 - P)Q.$$

This is the equation of a straight line, and it represents the best performance you can get with a system which acts on the strongest alternative indicated by two sources of evidence, and also picks the correct alternative if the two sources are in conflict. So if human beings worked in this way, then if we took a man who had one piece of information and added a gradually increasing amount of evidence from some other source, we would expect to find the probability of correct decision increasing gently in a way which was a constant fraction of the probability of

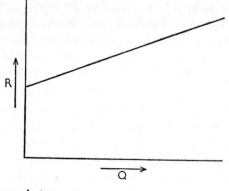

$$R = P + (1-P)\, Q$$

FIG. 1 The relationship between R and Q which is implied by an equation of the form $R = P + (1-P)Q$. Notice that as Q increases, R increases also, but not as much. It is this which makes random guessing a bad policy in many situations: one increases the frequency of one's successes only at the cost of increasing one's mistakes by a greater amount.

correct decision given the second source on its own. If Q gets bigger, R gets bigger too but not as much.

As an example of the other class of theory, consider Bayes' Theorem.

$$\frac{P_S}{1 - P_S} = \frac{P_N}{1 - P_N} \times \frac{P_C}{P_F}$$

To bring this into relation with the other equation, perhaps we ought to change P_S to R, P_N to Q, and P_C / P_F to X

$$\frac{R}{1 - R} = X \frac{Q}{1 - Q}$$

where X is a quantity related to the value of P. This equation has the property that, in certain parts of the range, R can change very drastically indeed when Q changes by quite a small amount. In other words, if a man operates on this basis, then as one adds some information from a second source, his probability of a correct decision may increase very sharply indeed. A small change in Q can give a big change in R.

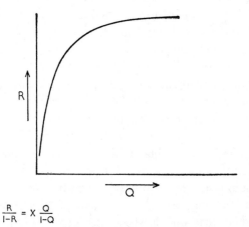

$$\frac{R}{1-R} = X \frac{Q}{1-Q}$$

FIG. 2 The relationship between R and Q which is implied by an equation of the form $R/(1-R) = XQ/(1-Q)$. Notice that when Q is small, a tiny change in it may give an enormous change in R. It is this which may make such a relationship very efficient: correct actions may be made much more frequent by a small change in the incidence of similar incorrect actions.

As this is fairly complicated, may I restate the key point at issue? One of my main themes throughout these Lectures is the importance in mental life of our own adjustments to the un-reliability of our brains and of the world at large. A second theme is the importance of the Bayesian approach, the consideration of hypotheses other than one's own favourite. When perception results in the accumulation of more than one kind of evidence, there are many ways in which this could be done, but in the extreme there are two main classes of mechanism which might combine evidence. One class of theory takes the correct decisions due to one source of evidence, and adds to them a certain proportion of the decisions which would be correct from the other source of evidence. This adding together is the type of thing you would expect if the system considered only the alternative most favoured by each source of evidence. On the other broad class of theories, a combination of two sources of evidence may give a very steep rise in combined performance as compared with that found when one source only is used. Mechanisms of this second type consider all the alternatives: and they will produce some occasions when correct performance will occur using both channels of information even although it would not have occurred with either on its own.

There are a very large number of experiments showing that evidence combines according to the second of these theories rather than the first. Just as an example, Endel Tulving of Yale and Irv Pollack of Michigan have studied the probability of correct identification of a word when one knows the context in which it appears, and also hears or sees it under rather difficult conditions (Tulving, Mandler and Baumal 1964: Pollack 1964). Suppose then that one looks at the probability of a correct identification of a particular word. For example, it may be very difficult to identify a word if told merely that it is preceded by the words 'Save the', and equally it may be quite difficult to identify the word if one knows nothing about its context but merely knows the first three letters. When told, however, that the sequence is 'Save the QUE', one can with a high certainty identify the word as QUEEN. Plotting the probability of correct recognition given both sources of information, against the probability given one only, they obtained a relationship which was markedly different from linear addition of probabilities. John Morton (1969a) has pointed out that it is rather of the form

$$\frac{R}{1 - R} = X \frac{Q}{1 - Q}.$$

There are many similar examples: but I want particularly to show that the principles of combination are such as to improve overall performance. To do this, it is best to take up again the question of probability which I mentioned in the previous Lecture. If we live in a world in which some things are more likely to happen than others are, then even though we perceive and act by adding up rather unreliable evidence, we can get a high level of objective success provided that we adjust suitably the criteria set in this cumulative or averaging mechanism. The reason is that a change in criteria can, thanks to the form of the mathematics, give a small change in errors but a large change in the number of correct percepts. The point I want to demonstrate in the rest of this Lecture is that we can use one source of information to change the criteria we set in reaching a decision about another source of information. To be concrete about it, suppose you are driving slowly in town, and are hailed from the sidewalk by somebody who calls, 'Hey, better stop; you've got a flat'. This information has a certain probability of being correct, which may well be less than perfect, especially if you know that your car is fitted with certain kinds of European tyre which look flat to Americans. One may therefore use ancillary information as a guide to the likely reliability of the source of this particular message. If for example it comes from a boy of about 10, who is laughing merrily while imparting it, and who furthermore is holding behind his back what looks rather like a couple of hub caps, you may perhaps decide that the information is likely to be in error. If on the other hand the information is imparted by a large gentleman of serious manner, who appears to be wearing the uniform of a State trooper, then even though he may still be incorrect, you are perhaps wise to act as he suggests.

First of all, let us consider again the effect of the probability of an event upon the accuracy with which it is perceived. We touched on this question in the previous Lecture, and you will remember that I mentioned that I had done some experiments on the perception of words which are common in the language and words which are less common. I also said that the probable words were more easily perceived, and that I could account for this effect entirely in terms of the difference in misperceptions which were common words: using a mathematical model based on the Tennis Theory. From what I have said in this Lecture, you will realize that the importance of using that theory is that it predicts a large effect on correct perceptions from a small difference in misperceptions: it predicts an equation of the type

$$\frac{R}{1-R} = X\frac{Q}{1-Q}$$

rather than one of the type

$$R = P + (1-P)Q.$$

Now I had some indirect evidence in my experiments that the perception of words does obey the first of these equations rather than the second, but this argument was a little indirect and would be invalid if, for instance, particular sounds were especially likely to occur in common words. I had not then demonstrated directly that small changes in the number of false perceptions of a word would indeed produce large changes in the number of correct perceptions of that word. One can, however, do so by applying to the perception of words a technique used in recognition memory by Egan (1958). Suppose that we show a man a word which is difficult to see: in fact we used a very poor carbon copy produced on a typewriter. When he has looked at it, then we show him a word which is completely clear and easy to read. We ask him whether the word which is shown is the same as the blurred one, or different. On half the occasions we do in fact give the correct word, and on the other half an incorrect word of the same probability in the language. When the man makes his judgment, we ask him to indicate his degree of confidence, and we thus get a whole set of judgments ranging from confident acceptances of the clearly visible 'probe' word to confident rejections of it, through various intermediate stages of uncertainty. If we take only the most confident acceptances, they are of course extremely rare when the probe word was in fact incorrect. They are rather greater when the probe word was correct. If we include also acceptances which are less confident we obtain more errors and also more correct judgments, and so on. We can thus obtain a complete curve relating correct acceptances to false ones, and we can see if the correct acceptances do indeed rise proportionally to the false acceptances.

The results are quite clear and unequivocal: if we call the probability of correct acceptance R, and the probability of a false acceptance Q, the results are approximately of the form

$$\frac{R}{1-R} = X\frac{Q}{1-Q}.$$

There are steep rises in the probability of correct acceptance when small increases in false alarm rate occur, and one could not possibly fit the results by an equation of the type

$$R = P + (1-P)Q.$$

Having thus shown the form of the relationship, one can then ask what is the effect of differences in word probability? If common words are particularly easy to see, this means that they have a larger value of R. But is this because they have a different value of X, or because they have a different value of Q? Do they lie on a different curve, or further along the same curve?

Once again, the result is quite clear. If one takes a sample of common words and a sample of uncommon words, without trying especially to balance the nature of the letters of which they are made, then common words do indeed differ in the value of X which they give. They lie on a different curve. But they differ by having a *smaller* value of X, and the curve lies below that for uncommon words. The greater ease with which common words can be seen is therefore entirely due to the fact that they have a higher value of Q than you would expect. If you are probed for a common word, you are more likely to accept it even if the evidence is less convincing. In fact it would seem that our language has so developed that common words are actually less distinctive in their visual shape than uncommon words are, so that the value of X is the wrong way round. This sheds quite an interesting light on language, but from the point of view of our present purposes, the important point is that the probability of an event is reflected in the tendency to perceive that event even in the absence of the appropriate stimulus, rather than in

E

greater sensitivity to the stimulus. This is the same message that I presented in the previous Lecture: there is no sign that perception is active, but rather that it is biassed but passive.

I am using this experiment to make several points: first, to show the kind of technique which one can use in this area, and also to show the sort of effects which probability has upon simple perception. In a moment, we shall go on to look at the effect of a second source of information. But notice particularly that the way human beings behave in such a situation is calculated to improve their success in life. They cannot become completely reliable machine-like systems, which always perceive with complete accuracy; but they can do better than they might if they adopted some other strategy. A bias towards the perception of probable events can give a very large increase in correct perceptions, at the cost of a smaller increase in false perceptions. This therefore is a sensible and rational strategy to adopt, which partly overcomes the unreliability of the perceptual system.

Now let us look more directly at the question of combining evidence, using a series of experiments devised by David Ingleby, formerly of Cambridge and now at the London School of Economics (Ingleby 1969; see also Broadbent 1971, p. 195). The problem which concerned him was the performance of a man who was listening for a sound which was difficult to hear. The man might, for example, be a maintenance engineer trying to detect a peculiar harmonic amongst the noise of an engine. As the sound was faint, the reliability of the man was low, and as an attempt to assist him he might be provided with a computer which would examine the sound mechanically and also decide whether or not a signal was present. The computer also however would be unreliable. The question is then whether the provision to the man of a visual indication of the opinion of the computer will change his performance, and if so in what way.

Before I tell you the results, let us think of the different ways in which the man might interact with the computer. First of all, I suppose he might simply ignore the computer, or else he might give up listening altogether and just do as the machine tells him.

In the former case, his performance would be the same whether there is a computer operating or not: and in the latter case his performance would be exactly the same as that of the computer. In fact neither of these happens; he makes more detections and fewer false reports when the computer is available than when it is not, so that the combination of man and machine does better than either on its own.

The second possibility is that the man might ignore the computer on a certain number of occasions, and follow it slavishly on the remaining occasions. For example, he might decide to report a signal whenever he hears it and in addition to report 50 per cent of the occasions when the computer says one is present but he has not heard it. A rule like this could certainly improve the probability of a correct perception, but only at the cost of increasing the number of false detections as well. More generally, suppose we do an experiment like the one on words of different probability, in which we ask the man to give his confidence about the presence or absence of a sound: so that we get a whole range of different values of false detections Q and their corresponding correct detections R. In the absence of any information from the computer we find as we might expect that

$$\frac{R}{1-R} = X \frac{Q}{1-Q}.$$

The procedure could be repeated for the case when a computer was present and was giving a visual indication, and for the case when a computer was present but was not indicating a signal. This will give three such curves: and if the man is performing by an additive combination of his own detections and detections by the computer, then these three curves cannot have the same value of X.

A third possibility is that the information derived from the computer might cause the man to listen with especial care when the computer thought a sound was present, and to relax and behave more randomly when the computer indicated that it was unlikely that anything was present. This is perhaps the sort of behaviour you might expect on an active theory of perception. It would imply once again that X would change between the three conditions of computer absent, computer present and indicating a signal, and computer present and indicating absence of signal.

Last of all, there is the fourth possibility that the computer will act by changing $Q/1 - Q$, but leaving X unchanged. This is the result to be expected if the computer information is being used to alter the criterion in some internal averaging process, rather than by competing with the evidence of the man's own ears, or by changing the intake of evidence from the ears.

We therefore have four possible kinds of behaviour of which the first has already been ruled out, the second and third predict changes in X from the presence of the computer, and the fourth predicts no change in X but a change in Q.

In Ingleby's situation the data support only the last class of theory. Whether a computer was present or absent, and whatever the indication of the computer was, one could plot the usual curve relating R and Q. The value of X was in each case the same: but when the computer thought a signal to be present, the values of R and Q were both increased, and when the computer thought the signal to be absent, they both decreased. We can therefore rule out several classes of theory of behaviour in this situation. We know that no additive theory can apply; that is, we know that the man is not ignoring the computer on some occasions and following it slavishly on others. Rather, he is combining the computer information with the evidence of his senses. We can also exclude theories which would suppose that the man uses the computer information to guide some active form of perception. We are left with the class of theories which supposes that the man alters the criterion in his internal averaging process, so as to increase the bias in favour of the conclusion to which the computer is pointing. There is a number of different kinds of theory which would have this general property, but it is a considerable gain to have cut down the possibilities to this group of theories. Notice also that this kind of mechanism is highly adaptive: by doing this the man will get substantially more correct detections and fewer false alarms than he would if he followed blindly his own senses or the judgment of the computer.

Let us look a little more closely at this question of the rational and adaptive nature of the performance. In the results I have mentioned so far, the computer was right about the presence of a signal on about 75 per cent of occasions. It also made about 25 per cent of false alarms, so that its probability of being correct was symmetrical both in reporting presence and in reporting absence of a signal. Signals occurred on half the trials, so the situation was symmetrical from that point of view also. In a different experiment, one could make the computer more or less accurate. If you do this, you find that the man takes more notice of the computer when it is reliable than when it is not. Another kind of experiment is to make the computer behave assymetrically, so that it is very cautious or very risky. If it is very cautious, then on most trials the computer will say no signal is present, and it will quite often be wrong. When, however, it does occasionally venture a judgment, it will be right on a high proportion of occasions. If one makes the computer work riskily, then it will report signals on a high proportion of trials, and will often be wrong: but when occasionally it refrains from reporting a signal, it will usually be right. If now we see how cautious or risky computers affect human judgment, we find that a cautious computer has a very large effect when it reports a signal, and a risky computer has a very large effect when it refrains from doing so: but each of them has rather little effect in the opposite condition.

Each of these results is broadly consistent with the behaviour one would expect from Bayes' Theorem. Remember the equation

$$\frac{R}{1-R} = X \frac{Q}{1-Q}.$$

On Bayes' Theorem, if Q is the probability of a hypothesis before we get evidence, and R is the probability after we have observed an event, then X is the likelihood ratio corresponding to that event. That is,

$$X = \frac{P_C}{P_F}$$

where P_C is the probability of the event if the hypothesis is correct and P_F is the probability of the event if the hypothesis is false. In our previous example, X was contributed by evidence at the senses, and the computer evidence is incorporated within $Q/(1 - Q)$. But all evidence is supposed to combine multiplicatively in the same way: if D is the contribution from the computer, and P is the *a priori* probability of reporting a signal in the absence of sensory or computer evidence, then

$$\frac{R}{1 - R} = X \, D \frac{P}{1 - P}.$$

Now we can say how D *ought* to change if the man is behaving as a rational statistician would. It is related to the likelihood ratio of the evidence provided by the computer, which we can call $1/\beta$. Then if we think of the output of the computer working symmetrically with a 25 per cent error rate, then $1/\beta = 3$. If the computer had an error rate of one third, then $1/\beta$ would be only 2, whereas if the computer had an error rate of one fifth, $1/\beta$ would $= 4$. Thus on Bayes' Theorem an increase in the reliability of the computer would give a greater likelihood ratio, and hence a bigger effect on the final decision about the presence of a signal. If the computer is very cautious, and reports only 16 per cent of signals with a low false alarm rate of 1 in a 100, then $1/\beta$ increases to 16 instead of 3, and a rational man would take far more notice of any report from such a cautious computer. In each case therefore the man is doing the right kind of thing to take advantage of the mathematical properties of the situation.

We have had a fairly heavy dose of mathematics, and I am afraid we are not quite finished yet, but let us have a breather by considering some of these phenomena in everyday terms. If you are trying to make up your mind about some complex issue, such as President Nixon's proposals for medicare in the United

States or the new Bill to regulate industrial relations in Britain, you probably do not have enough direct information to reach an accurate judgment. By studying the matter, you can make forecasts of the way you will be affected by such measures, and these forecasts will be right perhaps 60 per cent of the time. But you may also find that some noted public figure has a way of giving opinions which turn out, from your point of view, to be justified later by events at least as often as your unaided judgment. Perhaps what Spiro Agnew thinks today, you find you think tomorrow; or perhaps it is Professor Chomsky, or Milton Friedman, whom you find a good predictor. The opinion of this prestigious figure then will bias your own judgment; and the more often his opinion is confirmed by your own feelings in cases when you can look into the matter yourself, the more you will trust him in cases of doubt. Furthermore, you will be more swayed by a pronouncement from a man who rarely takes sides than by the opinion of the sort of over-exposed letter-signer who is always protesting about something. Ingleby's results on the relationship between a computer and a human listener apply roughly to your judgments in social situations. It is entirely reasonable that this should be so: life is short, information scarce and unreliable, and our judgments and experience faulty. By combining evidence and biassing our decisions in this way, we can attain a high rate of success and partially overcome our own limitations.

How near the ideal do we come? In Ingleby's experiments, the provision of a computer with a 25 per cent error rate should have increased $1/\beta$ by a factor of 3. The results of the experiments gave an increase, but not quite so large an increase as that. This is a general rule of such experiments: let me borrow an example from Ward Edwards of Michigan, in a modified form devised by Duncan Godden in Cambridge. Suppose you are in charge of a salvage operation searching for the wreck of a sixteenth-century Spanish treasure ship. Suppose also that you know that an English ship was wrecked in about the same place but that no other vessels are in the neighbourhood: if now you detect a wreck on your sonar, I hope you will agree that the probability of its being the Spanish one is 0·5. Now suppose we know that the Spaniard carried twice as many large cannon-balls as small ones, but the English ship only half as many large as small. You lower a grab, and pull up 9 small and 14 large cannon-balls; what now is the probability that the ship is Spanish? More than 0·5 obviously. But is it 0·6 or 0·7, or perhaps 0·8? Very few people will get the right answer. It is in fact 0·97.

This fact has been used as an argument against the idea that people combine evidence according to Bayes' Theorem; but I think wrongly. I will cite only one reason out of a number which make me think this: it rests on the fact that one can start from the man's performance and calculate what (if he was a Bayesian) he must have regarded as the likelihood ratio X corresponding to any evidence we give him. This subjective or inferred value of X is the same for the same evidence, even if the situation changes in other ways. Ingleby performed two experiments in which the reliability of the computer remained the same; but in one case the sound was made much more easily detectable by human hearing. This made the rate of correct detections depend much less on the presence of the computer; but nevertheless the effect of the computer in terms of inferred likelihood ratio was the same in both experiments. This is very strong evidence that people judge in terms of likelihood ratio; a given piece of evidence multiplies the odds on a given response by a constant amount, even though that amount may not be numerically the correct one.

Human beings do not perform therefore quite as well as a statistician would wish us to do, although in my view this is because our estimates of likelihood ratio are faulty. Furthermore, our very success at securing many correct perceptions may blind us to the heuristic and statistical nature of the process: we may imagine that these statistical judgments based on averages of unreliable impulses are completely trustworthy insights into objective reality. The Viscount pilot of my first Lecture was almost certainly led to over-read his altimeter by the unusual cloud conditions which were also present: a pilot can usually tell his altitude roughly from the cloud formations, but not every time, and once is enough to crash. In the social sphere, think of an experiment by Peter Warr of Sheffield, in which subjects judged the conduct of a priest involved in an episode described in a newspaper story. For half the subjects, the priest was described as an Episcopalian, for half as a Roman Catholic. Although the rest of the text was the same, the judgment of the priest's action was more favourable in each case for those subjects who thought he belonged to their own church (Warr and Knapper 1968). Clearly the predictor variable was being used far beyond its true value. In my country, exactly this particular bias is at this very time drawing a steady dividend of deaths and injuries, with each side sure of the truth of its own view of events.

Despite years of psychological effort, it is still not widely realized in our culture that a man can see something which did not happen, and that he does so precisely through the workings of the system which in other cases makes him perceive accurately. Experience is lawful, but unreliable, and *all* of us should remember at all times the possibility that we may be mistaken (Quote: O. Cromwell). We have no private door into reality; only a wonderful array of devices for making the best of an uncertain situation.

One last point for this Lecture: How can perceptual bias be overcome? The answer lies in the Bayesian equation

$$\frac{R}{1-R} = \frac{P_C}{P_F} \times \frac{Q}{1-Q}.$$

I have already laboured the point that this equation will give high accuracy with only small adjustments in Q. It is also true of this equation that large values of P_C can over-ride small changes in Q.

Suppose we have two alternative stimuli, which are almost impossible to distinguish so that only 50 per cent of perceptions are correct. If one stimulus is nine times more common than the other, a small bias of the perceptual criterion will raise the performance from 50 per cent to 82 per cent correct. But suppose this bias is present, and yet the stimuli are made more distinct so that 90 per cent of trials would be correct without the bias. Now the bias makes only 4 per cent difference. Clear and unambiguous evidence from the environment washes out the subjective bias, and we need not therefore despair of overcoming our own limitations.

You can see how all this connects with one of my general themes concerning scientific method: we need not take too seriously those who say that all judgment is biassed, that therefore there is no hope of reaching solid ground in the social sciences, and that experimentalists deceive themselves in seeking objectivity. Indeed bias is universal, for good and sufficient reasons. But the empirical and objective technique can still overcome these biasses: that is the whole point of pursuing it. In the next Lecture, I shall be considering the reasons for another tenet of Anglo-Saxon empiricism, the distrust of emotional language. I hope that the force of my data may overcome any bias you may have against so traditional a view.

4 The Use of
   Emotional Words

In Britain, our football teams have parties of supporters or fans who travel around with their teams by train; creating havoc on the train whenever their team loses. I sometimes toy with the thought that there might be similar fans for psychologists. Presumably if there were, they would get very indignant whenever they went to a meeting where their hero was stopped in the middle of his talk by a chairman belonging to some other university. This seems to me to be the obvious explanation for the fact that British Rail have decided to stop running trains between Cambridge and Oxford. Such an explanation has to me all the hallmarks of proof by the criteria of Sartre, summarized by Mary Warnock (1965) as 'a description so clear and vivid that, when I think of this description and fit it to my own case, I cannot fail to see its application'.

However, if there were psychological fans, and if there were some of them so ill-advised as to be fans of mine, they would perhaps have noticed that in the last few years my publication rate has been low. In particular, such papers as have appeared have often had the danger sign of being headed as by Broadbent alone, and not by Broadbent and Gregory. As many of you will know, Margaret Gregory and I have arrived at a division of labour such that she does the work and I talk about it: so that papers with only my name on them can safely be neglected since they contain only theory and no facts. My imaginary fans would doubtless have put this down to advancing years, to the cares of administration, and other similar causes, and begun to wonder about transferring their allegiance elsewhere. In fact, however, to quote Mountjoy, 'Though we seemed dead, we did but sleep; and advantage is a better soldier than rashness.' To put it another way, we have been engaged for some years in a series of experiments of which we could make no sense at all, and which therefore we did not dare to publish. Now at last the truth can be told. Of course, those who really know their Shakespeare will doubtless remind me that Mountjoy's king went on to lose the battle in the end, and there are features of this series of studies which make me fear the same fate. At least, however, I can now make a plausible story out of the results.

There are two reasons for telling this story. First, I want at this point in my argument to give an actual example of the way in which scientific knowledge grows, and of what is wrong with the kind of proof admired by existentialists. Briefly, enormous feelings of confidence about an interpretation are no guarantee of its viability; again and again the harsh stubbornness of data will check our most innocent assumptions. This fact is often masked by styles of journal reporting, although it is familiar to every working scientist. One has to reveal one's own mistakes if one wants to make the point.

The second reason for talking about this particular research programme is, however, its content. It has to do with the effects on perception of using emotional words. As I said in my previous Lecture, the classic style of Anglo-Saxon academics shuns such words. We strive for impersonal and neutral phrasing, turning sentences into the passive, toning down adjectives, and trying to be dull. Occasional voices are raised against this policy, and this has been particularly true lately. People begin to say that it is misleading to write 'The benefits of a slight under-use of productive resources are widely acknowledged to be substantial' when you really mean 'Chaps like me think some of the workers should have no job'. The argument is that the apparent neutrality allows one to exclude moral issues when these are nevertheless the most important ones. In the psychological sphere, R. D. Laing makes this point by example, describing the pressure which exists within a family to hold common values and attitudes by the term 'violence'. He also makes the point explicitly, saying that the choice of terms is a political act, and that violence cannot be seen through the sights of positivism. I myself disagree with this view: I think one should avoid the use of terms with a massive emotional charge. The point that moral issues ought to be discussed is a sound one, but using loaded words raises dangers which appear quite nicely in the experiments I am about to describe, and which underlie the traditional attempt at impersonality. The value to be attached to actual or potential facts ought to find its way into speech, but as a separate set of statements from those about the facts themselves.

Now, to turn to our research. There is a long established fact, with which the name of Professor Bruner of Harvard is of course connected, that people have trouble perceiving words which are uncongenial to them; in particular, obscene and socially unacceptable words. The fact has aroused a lot of research for two reasons; first, it may be connected with clinical phenomena labelled by words such as 'repression', in which a patient may be unaware of an interpretation of his own behaviour or motives which is glaringly apparent to those about him. This fact is therefore possibly a most important part of the processes of personal control over action. The second reason for concern with the phenomenon is that this particular mode of control seems to require a biologically unlikely kind of machinery, which offended many people on *a priori* grounds. It seems to mean that the part of the brain which analyses inputs from the environment, and which is presumably quite complicated, is preceded by another and duplicate part of the brain which carries out the same function, deciding what is there in order to reject or accept items for admission to the machinery which decides what is there. This seems so wasteful that one would like to avoid such a theory. Many people therefore criticized the experiments on the grounds that the emotional words were in fact less frequent in the experience of the experimental subjects (though the effect of word frequency itself requires explanation) or that perception took place but was followed by unwillingness to respond for social reasons. There are studies which overcome these objections to the satisfaction of many, but perhaps not of all. At this point the matter rested, when we became interested in it.

Our own studies had been concerned with the evaluation of telephone circuits, which we did using standard lists of words. We noticed that some words in these lists were much easier to hear than others were, and we wanted to remove this source of experimental error. Most of it was due to differences in the probability of the word in the language, so we started by examining that effect. It was quite obvious that misperceptions, as well as correct perceptions, were especially likely to be words common in the language. You will remember how I spoke in earlier Lectures of the totalling or accumulation of unreliable impulses until some critical level was reached, whereupon perception would occur. If the criterion demanded for a particular word was rather high, that word would be unlikely to occur as a misperception and also unlikely as a correct perception. So it looked as if the probability of a word in the language was affecting the criterion, less evidence being needed in favour of probable words. The interesting question, however, was whether the actual evidence coming into the perceptual system, the flow of impulses, was different as between probable and improbable words. On active theories of perception it might be, on passive theories it would not. We could test this by assuming that the evidence accumulated on a version of the familiar Bayesian formula

$$\frac{R}{1-R} = X\frac{Q}{1-Q}.$$

As I mentioned in the previous two Lectures, it turned out that the value of X, the evidence derived from the senses, was the same for common and for uncommon words; and in the latter Lecture I presented evidence that the Bayesian type of evidence combination does apply to words. It seemed, therefore, that we could explain the effect of probability on word perception entirely by the difference in criterion. But this is very attractive as a mechanism, because it means that the brain does not need one set of machinery to look at a word, identify it as a common word, and then pass it to a second set of machinery which identifies it again; rather there is a single system which makes up its mind in advance that it will need less evidence for certain kinds of word and thus makes the best use of its own unreliability. Suppose one could apply the same kind of explanation to the effects of word emotionality?

We therefore rushed out and did an experiment on the subject. The study has been published (Broadbent and Gregory 1967), but as it was the most complex experimental design I have ever undertaken I want to get full value out of it, and you must therefore put up with hearing it again.

First, take a set of sixty words of the same frequency of occurrence as determined by the Thorndike–Lorge count. Twenty of these are rather pleasant words, such as 'peace' or 'bed', twenty rather unpleasant such as 'blood' or 'death', and twenty rather neutral emotionally. In case your own judgment is peculiar, you march in a panel of Cambridge housewives, who rate each word on a seven-point scale for degree of unpleasantness. (In fact, Margaret Gregory made only one misclassification in assessing the words in advance.) You then record these words on magnetic tape against a noise background; but perhaps you have not spoken them with strictly equal intensity, since you yourself may be affected by the emotional words. Physical check is no good, because the dynamic range of speech is at least 30 dB, and in any case nobody knows which acoustic features of speech may carry the essential information in cases of this type. So you must check that the recording is equally good by trying another panel of housewives, who listen to the tape knowing what words are on it, but not knowing the order. It is known that 'forced-choice' conditions of this kind reduce the word-frequency effect markedly and probably that of emotionality, and even if any effect is left that will work *against* getting any effect in the main experiment. So it is fair to take words which are equal in forced-choice

69

performance and regard them as equally detectable physically. You have to throw out five words from each of your classes to achieve this, but that leaves you with forty-five words. You then bring in another group of housewives, whose results really form the main experiment, who listen to the tape without knowing what is on it, and write down what they hear. You then know the number of correct perceptions in each emotional class; and from the answer sheets you can collect all the misperceptions which were in the same frequency class as the original stimulus words. All these have to be presented to another group of house-wives who rate them for degree of pleasantness, so that you can tell whether the misperceptions are nice or nasty. Even then, you still do not know the relative number of nice or nasty words there may be in the language, which is important for the mathe-matics; so you take a random sample of words from the Thorn-dike–Lorge count in the appropriate frequency class, and give all those to a panel of housewives to be rated for pleasantness. At this point, one investigator says, 'Are we through?' and the other says, 'Let's do it again with a different frequency class of words.'

After all this, three simple facts emerged: first, unpleasant words are clearly and significantly harder to hear in both fre-quency classes, despite the fact that they are perfectly acceptable words socially, and despite the various precautions I have mentioned. Second, the absolute number of unpleasant words which occur as misperceptions is small. But, third, so is the number of unpleasant words in these frequency classes in the language; and the chance of any individual word occurring as a mispercep-tion is exactly the same whether it is pleasant or unpleasant. There is no sign whatever of a difference in criterion between emotional classes; and yet the number of correct perceptions of nasty words is low. Apparently when an emotional word is presented, some-thing unknown reduces the flow of evidence from the senses into the perceptual system. At least the effect cannot be due to word frequency, which *does* alter the rate of misperceptions; nor to the subject perceiving the word and then refusing to write it, which would presumably do the same. But nevertheless the result was a great disappointment.

Having published this odd fact therefore, we set out to try and explain it away. The position was not quite hopeless, because there were various points of doubt in our mathematics which needed examination. In particular, we wanted to check the possibility that the criterion for emotional words might be subject to larger variation than that for neutral words. This is psychologically very likely; it would mean that on some days experimental subjects might come in having slept well, got a raise in pay, and engaged to be married, and with words like 'Joy, peace!' bursting from their lips. On another occasion the same subject might have terrible indigestion, a recent quarrel with her husband, and with her shoes hurting. Words like 'Death, rage!' might then seem more appropriate. Neutral words on the other hand might not be liable to these ups and downs. But our mathematics had assumed equal variability for both kinds of words, and this might conceivably have produced our results. If we were going to check this possibility, we needed to be sure that the physical stimuli for nasty words were the same as those for neutral ones, not only in average but also in variance. This was really too much for the forced-choice method of matching spoken words, so we decided to go to visual stimulation and use written words, which would not be contaminated by the weaknesses of a human talker. But we still wanted to test large numbers of people, which means group testing. So we set out to use the following technique, which resembles one used earlier in other people's research, and which we employed for the first five of the experiments I want to describe.

We prepared slides of each word from the list we had previously used in hearing, but this time typed out. Each slide was then projected on a screen, with the projector thrown out of focus by a deliberate amount so that it was difficult to make out the word. It remained visible for five seconds, and each of the group of subjects wrote down what she thought the word was. We had previously shown that similar methods would give the usual word-frequency effect. Imagine therefore our surprise to discover that our first study on emotional words, which I may call Projector 1, gave no difference between neutral and nasty words.

After a little thought, it occurred to us that the slides had been prepared with a manual typewriter, and possibly the typist had hit the keys with extra vigour when typing nasty words. So in Projector 2, we had all the words retyped with an electric typewriter. Still no luck at all. By now rather aghast, we remembered the fact that I mentioned in the previous Lecture, that common words actually have less discriminable letters in them. Perhaps the same is true for neutral words, so that one really needs to equate the words by forced-choice even in vision. We therefore did a forced-choice study, Projector 3. Still no difference between neutral and nasty words.

At this stage experiment having failed, I decided it was necessary to start thinking. We began to list systematically some of the things we knew could affect the perception of words, and which might be present in one or other of our classes. The first such factor is frequency in the language, which like most other investigators in recent years we had already controlled. The second factor is length of word, which in these projector experiments we had not controlled exactly. The reason was that we were using the same words as in the acoustic experiment, and they were equivalent in spoken length; but this does not mean that they have the same number of letters. In this we were distinctly inferior to most other people in this field, and obviously we ought to do something about it. Thirdly and more interestingly, there is the question of the nature of the initial letter of the word. Moishe Anisfeld, of Harvard, has shown that people asked to write down nasty words tend to produce words starting with certain letters: these letters are somehow themselves nasty (Anisfeld 1968). A look at most previous studies of the subject will show that their nasty stimulus words also tend to start with such letters, whereas ours did not. Perhaps the mechanism of the effect is for the perceptual system to detect the first letter of the word, find that it is nasty, and promptly switch itself off. Our particular words would not have produced such a result; though perhaps when heard rather than seen these same words might have some other cue which gave the same effect.

The fourth possible factor is related to the frequency of the word. Not only the word itself is characterized by a probability in the language, but so also is the sequence of letters which makes it up. You can find common words which have uncommon sequences of letters, and uncommon words with common sequences, although of course common words are likely to have common sequences. As I said in Lecture 2, we had had a look at the perception of such words, trying to see whether common letters tended to be particularly easy to see even in uncommon words. I said the results were unsatisfactory; the reason was that we found rare letter sequences actually helped the perception of uncommon words, which no theory of perception predicted. But if one looks at previous studies of emotional words, one does find that the emotional words are sometimes made up of rare sequences of letters even though the word itself is controlled in frequency. So perhaps that ought also to be matched between neutral and emotional words.

Fifth, there is a factor which I regard as especially important; the size of the set of words similar to the stimulus. Let me explain this by taking the stimulus word 'ten'. Suppose that word is exposed and you see only the first and last letters. It could be 'tan' or 'tin', or 'ton' spelt two different ways, as well as 'ten'. But the loss of the middle letter from the word 'let' allows only two different wrong answers, 'lit' and 'lot', the other vowels producing sequences which are not words. In the extreme case, the loss of one letter from the word 'Popacatapetl' still leaves it almost impossible to find any other word which fills the remaining requirements. This factor is related to the rarity of the sequence of letters making up the word, and in fact we have found that our uncommon words with rare sequences of letters also have very few other words which are similar to them; which I now think to be the reason for their being easy to see (Broadbent and

73

Gregory 1971). Anyway, this factor also ought to be controlled in any comparison of neutral and nasty words.

We therefore assembled a new vocabulary of words, which controlled all these factors, and we ran Projector 4 to see what happened. With the benefit of these careful experimental controls, we had now managed to make the nasty words *easier* to see than the neutral ones. Just to make sure, we used the new words in a probe experiment similar to that used for word frequency in the previous Lecture; which still gave no advantage for neutral words. We then retired to lick our wounds.

There were at this stage three possibilities. One was that the whole effect was nonsense; that really there is no effect of the nastiness of a word, and that we had happened to get some unlucky sample of recordings in our acoustic experiment which had produced an artefact. I was reluctant to believe that, not only because of the amount of work we had invested, but also because our acoustic experiments did have quite a number of precautions in them which I described, and because other people have (as I said) got effects of emotionality with experiments which seem to me watertight. The second possibility therefore was that there is a difference between vision and hearing; you can turn off your ears but not your eyes. This is not as silly as it sounds, because the physiological evidence for control of the ear by efferent fibres is much better than it is for the eye. But it was a low probability, because of the results of previous workers with vision.

The third possibility was that there was some other difference between our visual and auditory experiments, apart from the sense being stimulated. Looking at the two tasks, there is one possibility, which has to do with the length of time for which the stimulus remains available to the subject. In the projector experiments it was there for five seconds, whereas a spoken word goes past in a third of a second or less. Just conceivably, time might be important in the effect of emotionality. At any rate, it was worth excluding the possibility by setting up an experiment in which visual stimuli were present for only a short time, and this we set out to do.

We used very brief exposures in this new series of studies, rather than a blurred projection, and therefore we called them Tach (for tachistoscopic). In the first experiment we employed our new balanced words typed in lower case, and for each subject determined an exposure duration at which she could see some of the words but not all. Then we gave the series of test words at that duration, and looked to see whether nasty and neutral words were equally easy to see. At last, we had got back to the results we found in hearing; nasty words were harder to see. I must admit that when we repeated this experiment, Tach 1a, by using upper-case lettering, we lost the effect again (Tach 1b) and I can only explain that result by thinking that the subjects tended to revert to looking at the words letter by letter when faced with capital letters. This would be reasonable when words have no clear shape, and is partly supported by an indication that nasty letters were harder to see in this case. Anyway, we were not too perturbed, and thought we ought to try a different set of words, in lower-case type, to see if we went on getting the effect. This we did in Tach 2, using the original words from the acoustic experiment, mixing together both high frequency and low frequency words in order to get a goodly number of words.

Up to a point, all went well in Tach 2. We did find that neutral words were seen more often than nasty ones, among the common words. Thus we had two visual results now in the same direction as our auditory ones, whereas in the projector experiments we never got anything. However, there was still one odd point; in Tach 2 the effect did not occur among the uncommon words, despite the fact that in hearing we had got the result both with common and with uncommon words. Looking at the details of the experiment, we noticed that our randomization procedure had let us down: it so happened that the uncommon nasty words tended to be preceded by neutral ones and vice versa. So the neutral ones were being tested when the subject had just seen a nasty word, but the nasty words were being tested in another condition. On reflection this did not seem a very good idea, although most other investigators do not say that they have worried about it; so we took the low frequency words, both neutral and nasty, and made up a new sequence in which each subject had half her nasty words preceded by neutral ones and half by nasty; and the same for her neutral words. Over the whole group of subjects, any particular word occurred as often preceded by a neutral word as by a nasty one. This study we called Tach 3.

At this point we hit the jack-pot, because we found nasty words were harder to see than neutral ones. Remember that these were the same words which had failed to show an effect in Tach 2, being presented in the same way excepting only that the order of presentation was different. So this result made two points with one blow. First, in a word perception experiment the state of the subject is changed in some way by having had a nasty word on the previous trial. Second, when this factor is controlled and when one uses tachistoscopic presentation, one can get a difference between neutral and nasty words. Thus far we have had three results where this is the case, and, to anticipate, we have also done Tach 4 in which we got the effect again, so it seems reasonably reliable. The effect of emotionality on word perception depends on the stimulus being available only for a short time.

This by itself does not help us with the problem of the mechanism of the effect; but the very fact, that nasty words have an after effect which hangs on until the arrival of the next word, gives one a way into the problem. What change might the perception of nastiness induce in a person? As it happened, there was other work going on in our lab on the effects of noise and other stresses on performance. For various reasons, people studying noise nowadays believe that one of its effects is to induce in human beings a general state which is similar to that which people enter if they are under a strong incentive: excited or aroused. There are four different lines of experiment which show this, which I need not enumerate here having done so on p. 429 of Broadbent (1971); for our purposes, the only thing that matters is the conclusion that the effects of noise might possibly have something in common with those of having just seen an emotional word. One of the effects of noise is to produce a change in the distribution of attention between different sources of information. Bob Hockey of Cambridge had been studying this, using a task in which a man was faced simultaneously with a tracking task and a detection task. In the centre of his field of vision there was a moving pointer, which he had to follow by moving another pointer through a long hand-lever. Arranged in an arc out to each side of the field of vision there were faint signal lights, and while he was tracking one of these lights might come on. If so, he had to report the fact. The lights in the centre of the field were much easier to see, being nearer to the tracking task, and correspondingly the man saw more of them; and although signals came objectively just as often from the edge of the field as from the middle, he thought there were fewer at the periphery. (This, rather than position on the retina or anything of that sort, has been demonstrated by Hockey to be the crucial difference between the different signal sources so far as noise is concerned.) What happened in noise was that the normal bias towards detecting lights in the easier positions was exaggerated; the lights at the periphery of the field were even less frequently detected, but those in the centre positively improved. Noise seems in fact to produce a kind of funnel vision, increasing the use of that part of the displayed information which is itself already receiving the greatest attention (Hockey 1970).

How might a similar effect show itself in the perception of words? If we look at misperceptions, we usually find that they resemble the stimulus in one or more letters; the observer does not come out with some misperception unrelated to the stimulus, but rather detects accurately some letters and makes errors on others. Suppose we look at misperceptions and count the number of occasions when *both* the first and the last letter were correct. These one might call 'wide angle errors' or something of that sort; the subject has clearly taken in information from spatially separated parts of the visual field. They can be contrasted with 'funnel vision errors', in which two letters adjacent to each other, including one of the end letters, were correct, but the other end letter was *not* correct. Now one can look at the difference in the

77

number of wide angle and of funnel vision errors in Tach 3, when the stimulus word was preceded by a neutral or by a nasty word. This analysis repays the effort; funnel vision becomes significantly more common when the previous word was nasty. Remember too that in Tach 3 the same stimulus words occurred equally often with each kind of preceding word, so that the nature of the stimulus itself was controlled. It certainly looks therefore as if the nastiness of one word is changing the strategy adopted by the subject in extracting information from the next word; but of course we found this feature of the data only after it had been collected, and rather in the spirit of finding a *post hoc* explanation for our results of other kinds. So we thought it as well to carry out Tach 4, which was like Tach 3 but used the other set of stimulus words. The results were the same; an effect of emotionality of a word both upon the detectability of that word itself and also upon the relative incidence of funnel vision errors on the next word. Looking back at the projector experiments, however, there was no sign of an increase in funnel vision errors following nasty words: and one can see why not. Given five seconds to brood over a blurred word, the subject can peer first at one end of the word, then later at the other, and his errors may perfectly well contain correct letters from both ends even though his strategy of information gathering is completely 'funnel vision' at any instant.

Those are all the facts I have to offer; I know now that our projector experiments did not work because of the long exposure of the stimulus, and I know that any future studies must control the nature of the preceding word. I also know that the nastiness of a word does make it harder to see as well as to hear, provided one watches one's technique sufficiently carefully. Furthermore, that difficulty still has nothing to do with changes in the relative numbers of neutral and nasty misperceptions; throughout these studies we have been checking on that point, and there are no indications of anything at all in the misperceptions. After all this work, therefore, we have not arrived at a solution to the problem we had four years ago: why is the intake of evidence from nasty words less than that from neutral ones? All we have established is that the effect is utterly different from that of word frequency. But the odd and unexpected fact, that each word affects the state of the person when they perceive the next one, changes my own attitude to the problem in such a way as to make it less worrying.

You will remember that the disturbing feature of the effect is that it seems to require a duplication of mechanisms. But a theoretical description in which this is so is a static one, leaving time out of account. The effect of one word upon the next is, on the contrary, a dynamic effect in which the state of the person has been changed. We are not entitled to say that the after-effect upon the next word is the same in nature as the effect upon the word itself; it might logically be different and mediated by some other mechanism. Notice that I was unable to say that a nasty word made the next word harder to see, nor that a nasty word tends itself to give rise to funnel vision errors; the two effects might be different. There is, however, the tempting resemblance that each of them depends upon tachistoscopic presentation. Furthermore, once one starts to think in terms of systems which change with time, one goes on thinking in that way.

Consider then a different kind of perceptual system, in which there is only one mechanism for analysing the nature of the stimulus, but in which the output of that mechanism feeds back to the mechanism itself in such a ways as to change its parameters. This after all is what is happening on a slow scale when one word affects the perception of the next. But suppose that the identification of a word as nasty then produces an emotional state which changes the strategy of intake of information so as to give 'funnel vision'. This in turn might change the identification of the stimulus, which would change the state of the mechanism, and after an oscillation or two such a dynamic system would settle down to a final value which might be less likely to be correct than the output of the same system without the interfering emotional state. It would only then be necessary for the output of the first system to be followed by a 'low pass filter' or further process of averaging which removed the very brief occurrence of the correct output from any chance of emerging into observable behaviour. As you will recall, I have all kinds of other reasons for wanting to postulate the existence of two successive processes of averaging or cumulation. So this seems to me quite a plausible mechanism, and it does not raise the problem of duplication of facilities within the brain.

However, this is speculation, which in turn suggests further experiments. For the purposes of my larger argument, I want to draw a few general lessons from this saga. First, notice that repeatedly our obvious expectations and confident beliefs failed to stand the test of confrontation with data. The immediate appeal of a theory is no guarantee of truth; and we can check it only by a flow of information from our environment, which means by experiment. Secondly, notice what happens to people when emotional words are used. They develop funnel vision; they collect information predominantly from one region of the environment which happens to be dominant, and neglect other sources which are also available. In other words, emotional excitement is precisely the state in which you are least likely to break the embrace of your plausible theory, and this is the reason for the stuffy and impersonal tone of our academic journals. It is essential to remember the moral implications of economic policy or of the family structure present in one's culture; but if one wants to change it, the use of emotionally loaded words is exactly the way least likely to have any impact except upon those who already agree with you. It is also a good way of rendering yourself unlikely to notice the slant which the traditions of your society or your own personal needs may give to your own perception.

So much then to justify my attitude to science and to politics, which as I said in the previous Lecture I know to be that of my sub-culture. What about the picture of human nature we have been building up? We have added to the simple chain of averaging or cumulating processes a control over the admission of information decided by the state of the system itself, and also we have added an effect of the past. To track the origins of the impulses to action we are going to have to look therefore at the residue of the past, the stored information within the system. Upon that depends not merely the action taken upon present information, but even the nature of the information taken in. In the next Lecture I shall be looking at the organization of memory.

5 The Recall of
   Particular Memories

In the previous Lectures, I have built up a picture of the choice of actions as the result of a gradual accumulation of impulses pointing in different directions, but on average favouring one outcome. For most of the series of Lectures, however, I have talked as if the only source which produces these impulses is the outer world. I have in fact fallen back into the experimental psychologist's usual trap, of discussing perception as if it were the whole of mental life. The reason we do this is simply that perception is the easiest topic to study in the laboratory; and I do not think one need apologize too much for that, because we can find out in that field important principles which often apply elsewhere. From the previous three Lectures, I hope you will have gathered some important points about the way in which impulses are accumulated or averaged, the effects of emotional states, and so on. But all the same, in adult human beings the dominant cause for many actions arises within the man himself and not in his present surroundings. The quantity of information stored within each person is enormous, and it may emerge in many unexpected circumstances. Within myself, there is still a record of the day thirty years ago when I stood out on a football field and watched German bombers pounding the centre of Southampton into rubble. Perhaps more vividly still, I recall the intellectual problems which adolescents debated at that time. As we realized, had we been born 600 miles to the east, we too might have thought the destruction of cities or the extermination of Jews to be valuable stepping-stones to human progress. If, therefore, these men had absorbed their values from their culture, and we ours from our own, in what sense could there be any absolute standard of comparison? And why was it that, in full awareness of this intellectual difficulty, we nevertheless felt intuitively that the divergence of the two cultures was more than merely trivial, and that adherence to or rejection of one of the two sides was an intensely important moral choice? It really does make a difference what the inside of a man's head is like. It is easy to see in these events of the distant past the origins of the concern I have been showing throughout these Lectures with problems of cultural determination and individual responsibility.

In general terms, that is all very well. But there is an immense amount of information within my head, extracted from forty-odd years of experience: why does some of it govern behaviour at one time, and other parts at another time? Why did I recall that football field when writing this Lecture, rather than my first sight of Professor Boring or of Anna Freud? The baffling feature of these internally arising signals is not simply that they store some representation of the past: but that out of all the many representations of the past, one particular one is selected.

Let me illustrate the problem of memory by an analogy which I experienced some years ago. I went away from my lab for a year on leave, and occupied a pleasant suite of rooms in Oxford. A few letters began to arrive for me there, and I tossed them one after another into a drawer. At first all was well, but then it gradually emerged that my only way of finding a past letter was to look at about the right date for it: and if I did not happen to know the date, I had to look through all the letters I had received. So within a month or two I had to reorganize the system alphabetically by authors, since I was more likely to know the author of the letter than its date. Gradually that too became insufficient, because there might be very many letters from people whose names began with a certain letter. Furthermore, the correspondence on a certain topic such as a research grant application might be dotted about between various authors, and it was difficult to assemble a complete story. Consequently, I would start keeping a separate collection of letters dealing with research grant applications, with the bundle for each application clipped together. All these devices, which most of you will know from your own experience, served the purpose not merely of preserving the letters, but of arranging them so that I could find the particular letter wanted, when some message reached me which called for it. Each successive system I adopted made it easy to find some letters, and hard to find others. The ones which were hard were, from my point of view, effectively lost and I might as well not have kept them. By the time one has three or four filing cabinets full of mail, it is no help to be sure that some crucial information is in a certain letter in those files, if you do not know who signed the letter and therefore cannot locate whereabouts it is.

This problem of retrieval is a crucial one in all systems of stored information, whether they are files, libraries, computer memories, or our own memories. Formally speaking, the problem is one of selecting out of the information store one particular segment which contains the desired item. A large number of different means can be used to carry out this selection, and are used in libraries, files, and computers, just as in my own personal collection of correspondence. In the case of human memory, the importance of the problem has been largely emphasized by Endel Tulving at Yale, and some of the experiments I shall be quoting later also demonstrate it. But in many ways the problem is logically obvious once it has been pointed out: there are many things in memory, so what decides the one which controls action on a particular occasion?

Let us think about the ways in which problems of retrieval can show themselves in memory. The field is nowadays very complicated, and simply to save time I should like to refer you to two recent surveys I have written of the literature (Broadbent 1970a; Broadbent 1971, Chapter VIII). But for present purposes I want to concentrate on the effects on memory of combining two or more paths for retrieval. If something is in memory but temporarily lost, must we search for one vital trigger to release the memory, or can several factors combine? Did I recall 1940 because many different features of this situation pushed me towards it, or simply because there was one predominant factor which was dominant over all others?

An experiment on this point has been carried out by Peter McLeod and Caro Williams, who were at the time undergraduates at Cambridge. The technique was to deliver a list of words and then to get the subject to recall as many of them as he could. He only succeeded of course on a certain proportion of the words. Now Tulving has shown that one can produce recall of such words by giving the subject a hint, in the shape of a word which is related to the desired word (Tulving and Osler 1968). For each word in the list used by McLeod and Williams, the experimenters provided themselves with two other words which were known from free association experiments to give the desired word as an associate, and yet which did not often give each other as associates. To take an example which was not actually used, the word 'BLUE' might not call up to you the word 'ROUGH', and yet each of those words might summon up the word 'SEA'. When McLeod and Williams had got a subject to recall as many words as he could, they found out which words had been forgotten, and for each such word they gave one of the hint words. This prompting produced a substantial further number of recalls. Still, however, there were a few more words unrecalled, and again a second hint was given for each of these. This second hint produced a further crop of recalls.

The question now arises, how does the probability R of recalling with two hints relate to the probabilities P and Q of recalling with each of the hints separately? We find straight away that when we present the second hint, considering only those words which have not already been recalled, our chances of success are greater than they were when we presented the first hint. In other words, having two hints working together gives better performance than would be expected from the equation

$$(1 - R) = (1 - P)(1 - Q)$$

or to put it another way, two hints together will elicit some correct recalls which could not have been produced by either hint alone. You will perhaps not be too surprised to hear me say that the nearest mathematical model to the actual data (although still not a perfect fit) was a model of the type

$$\frac{R}{1-R} = X\frac{Q}{1-Q}.$$

Thus in getting at information from inside the man, as well as in securing perception of the environment, an equation of the type of Bayes' Theorem seems to hold. The portion of the past which comes up is found only in a rather unreliable fashion by any one cause alone, but by two or more factors in combination a highly determinate result can be produced. The filing system in our brains is cross-indexed to find a particular memory rather than storing it under only one heading (McLeod, Williams and Broadbent 1971).

But if this is the way in which different systems of retrieval interact, it seems fairly clear that the same principle does not apply throughout the whole field of memory. Again I will refer you to reviews of the area, but in brief, factors which increase the probability of recall of the tenth word in a list of 40 have no effect on the recall of the 39th word. This is one of the pieces of evidence which in my view mean that one cannot think of a single memory system. I think rather one has to distinguish two rather separate systems, one of which handles the great bulk of past experience, and within that system different retrieval features can be used in combination. The second memory system applies only to the last five or six events to be experienced. In that system, retrieval is on a basis of recency, and hardly any other features are available for that purpose. Thus there is quite a sharp distinction between the two systems, such that I would really regard them as being two separate kinds of memory.

In terms of the analogy of my personal files, I think we have to distinguish a Filing Cabinet in which letters are arranged by author or perhaps by topic, and an In-Basket in which the last few letters to arrive are still sitting before they are extracted and placed in the file. In the file, it is of very little relevance how long ago the letter was received but only how well it was indexed. Correspondingly the signature or the topic of the letter have little effect on the probability of finding it in the In-Basket. A rather similar system is to be found in most libraries, where there is a shelf for recent acquisitions, from which a book is later taken to be placed on the shelves organized by subject matter and by author.

We have therefore distinguished a short-term from a long-term memory, and in doing so I am in harmony with many other contemporary psychologists. But is this distinction enough, or must we complicate the picture even more? I am afraid I do want to do so, although this puts me at odds with many other theorists of memory. You will want to be spared some of our technical disputes, but the modification I want to introduce into the particular technical question of memory has a lot to do with the more general question of control of human actions, and therefore with the questions of freedom and responsibility to which I promised you that my whole argument was going to lead. So I ought to explain what the modification is, even though I shall only give one or two pieces of evidence for my dissatisfaction with merely two memory systems.

Let me first explain my point in terms of my analogy of the Filing Cabinet and the In-Basket. When I am actually conducting a day's work, it is not sufficient simply to plough through the incoming mail that has arrived that morning, because it may be desirable to do some jobs which have nothing to do with any correspondence from the In-Basket, but rather refer to items in the main files. For example, I ought really to write and inquire why I have heard nothing about a letter I wrote two weeks ago, or perhaps I ought to initiate some proposal for which I have all the background evidence in previous correspondence, but which will not be provoked by any stimulus from the outside world. To deal with this kind of situation, I may add to my Filing Cabinet and my In-Basket some notes on my desk top. These notes are simply to remind me to look in certain places to get the information to do the necessary jobs: they may say for example, '1. Has Bloggs replied? 2. Are you going to ask for an equipment allocation on the best of those estimates? 3. Answer today's mail'. Each note therefore does not contain enough information for me to do the job concerned, but rather sends me to the appropriate section of the file, or to the In-Basket, to get the information I need.

Similarly, I suspect that human memory contains three components rather than two. There is a separate store (the In-Basket) for the last five or six events which have occurred, and if one wants one of those events one simply looks at the entire In-Basket. There is also a separate store for events in the more remote past (the Filing Cabinet), which is organized and indexed in a complicated fashion so that one can locate particular events out of the whole array. Thirdly, however, I also believe that there is something corresponding to the Desk Top: namely, a small set of stored entities which I shall call addresses. By 'addresses' I mean that each entity does not consist of a complete event, but rather of sufficient information to locate the complete event in one of the other stores. I would believe that the number of these addressess held in readiness at any one time is limited, and this has effects on the total number of items which can be recalled from any one list. The limit does not take the form of a constant number of words or events which can be recalled, because each address may select more than one event: to revert momentarily to the analogy of my correspondence files, I can have several letters dealing with a certain topic. Correspondingly, as a list of words presented for memory is increased, there is a constant probability for each extra word that it can be added to one of the addresses already in play.

You see why this modification is relevant to my general line of thought. If we jump right back to the first Lecture, we can see a parallel between the command signal for a visible action and the address of an item or a complex of inter-related items in memory. An action is not a particular set of movements, and

88

equally the address of a memory is not the contents of the memory itself. But the list of addresses held in play at any one time can produce a sequence of actions each dependent primarily upon information stored within the man. (You will recall that in the first Lecture I noted that the distinction between behaviour of human beings such as language, and behaviour of insects such as reproduction, did not lie in structural properties, but rather in the degree to which they were determined internally rather than externally.) If my view of the system is correct, the set of addresses will provide a basis for long sustained actions independent of environmental support; and in turn the form that action shall take will be decided by the employment of a particular system of addressing. I recalled 1940 in this Lecture rather than my first encounter with some great psychologist, because my mind is not organized in a way which makes air raids and political systems irrelevant intrusions on the pure niceties of science. On the contrary, I would hold that, if warfare is the continuation of diplomacy by other means, then equally there is a sense in which science is the continuation of warfare by different techniques. That is, it is a means of deciding between attitudes and interpretations of the world, by certain procedures. It has the advantage over warfare, however, that it is not restricted to eliminating the opposing point of view, but may convert people with their full and willing consent. I would certainly, however, classify my activities in the laboratory as part of a framework which includes the era of armed resistance to Fascism. Returning from that digression, let us just make the point that the system of addressing or classification used by any person would tend to affect the particular course of action he will pursue.

To become yet more specific, what evidence is there really for retrieval as an important source of difficulty in recall? I have mentioned of course Tulving's experiments on the beneficial effects of a hint, and that of McLeod and Williams. But according to my general ethos I ought to look for alternative explanations, and there is at least one obvious possibility. Since we are always talking about words in English, which are in some sense already present in memory even before any experiment is started, we must be discussing some kind of stored information which is associated with each word and which indicates that it was indeed present on this particular occasion. Let us call this stored information the 'strength' of the word. Then presentation of the item increases its strength, and it might be also that the giving of a hint increases its strength as well, in such a way that the two increases of strength were sufficient to reach some threshold value and produce recall. In this kind of way, the availability of a hint could produce recall of words which would otherwise be inaccessible, and one need not then suppose any additional method of locating the right words. However, a suitable experiment to exclude this possibility has been carried out by two more undergraduates at Cambridge, Miss Wingrove and Mr Giddings. What they did was to present a list, and then to follow it by a mixture of words from the list and of words which had not been presented. The subject was then asked to recognize the ones which had been on the list. Provided that a word is seen and understood in the same sense in the recognition test as in the original presentation, it is not clear that there should be any problem of retrieval whatever in a recognition test.* There will, however, be a problem of the strength of trace, and this will be reflected in the fact that some of the original words will not be recognized, while some of the completely new words will be falsely accepted as having been presented earlier.

Suppose now that in the recognition test one accompanies half the words of each category by a hint, which in a recall experiment would improve performance. If such hints were to increase strength indiscriminately, one might expect to find that words accompanied by a hint would be accepted more often whether they were old or new. On a different form of strength model, one could suppose that the hint would increase the strength of words which already had a little extra strength from earlier presentation but would make no difference to those which had never occurred before. Neither of these things happens. There

* The first clause of this sentence is crucial: see, e.g. Light and Carter-Sobell 1970.

appears to be no effect of hints in recognition, despite the repeated finding that they have a beneficial effect in recall. The advantage of the hint is therefore quite clearly in locating a word and not in increasing its strength.

The argument thus far shows only that retrieval is improved by prompting from the environment. This does not show, however, that a man recalling without any hints or outside stimuli is working on some internal set of retrieval addresses. One could imagine yet another variant of the strength model, on which items spontaneously recalled would be so because they had a greater strength, and that if the strength was insufficient for recall it might nevertheless be enough to secure adequate recognition if a particular word was selected and its strength observed. The selection could then occur either because the word itself was presented, or because a hint was given and the man ran through in his head all the possible associates of that word. Nevertheless, it might be that spontaneous recall depended upon strength. To disprove this, I want to describe an experiment which is larger in scale than those mentioned previously, and is perhaps the major one to be reported in this Lecture. The purpose of the study is to look at the differences between items which are freely recalled, without any hint or prompting, and those which are not.

First of all, we carry out an experiment of the type described previously, in which a man receives a list of words and is asked to remember them. The words are printed out in front of him on a teletype. At the end of the list, he is asked to recall as many words as he can, in any order and they are typed back into the teletype. As the words are being presented by a computer, the responses of the subject can be scored immediately, so that when he finishes recalling he can at once be given a recognition test which contains all the words which he has seen but failed to recall, together with an equal number of new words, the whole being mixed in a random order.

It is of course very reasonable to find that the man does quite well at this task of recognizing words he has already failed to recall. That would be expected from the results already talked about, and on any of the theories we are discussing. On the strength theories, even though the old words have insufficient strength to secure recall, they may still have a greater strength than the new. What we really want to know, however, is whether the words which were recalled were stronger still, or whether their recall was due to some quite different cause, such as the availability of an address which allows them to be located in the memory.

There are several different comparisons we can make to shed light upon this. First of all, we can simply present another list, and give a recognition test for every item. Since at least some of the items would have been recalled, it must then follow that we have in effect tested a mixture of recalled and non-recalled items, and if the strength of the recalled items were greater we would expect this recognition test to give better performance than the test carried out only on forgotten items.

In fact, one needs to be just a little cautious about the comparison, because, when the recognition test is given immediately, each item is being tested at a short interval since presentation, and with few intervening events. When the test follows recall, the retention interval is longer and filled with activity. Unless one is sure therefore that performance of the recognition test is unaffected by these factors, we ought really to compare performance after the same retention interval: roughly speaking, the attempt at recall took about half as long as the retention test, so this means that one should compare only the second half of the unselected recognition test, with the first half of the test for forgotten items. If we make that comparison, then recognition is just about as efficient in either case, and there is certainly no significant difference.

This is a little unsatisfactory, because there was indeed a change in recognition test performance with time, so that if we had not been careful about picking particular parts of the recognition test, the result would have been different. It is also a little doubtful whether it is quite the same thing to spend a given length of time trying to recall on the one hand, or doing a recognition test on the other. So we did another experiment, in which we compared recognition for forgotten items with recognition for the whole list. Whereas forgotten items were tested after a period spent in recall, the whole list was tested following a corresponding period spent trying to think of as many words as possible which contain a prescribed number of letters (different from the length of the words in the memory list). This experiment also gave no difference between forgotten items and the whole list.

All this suggests quite strongly that there is no difference on average between the items which are recalled and the items which are not, and therefore that recall depends on something other than the strength of the item. This is really almost too good to be true, because one would quite reasonably have expected some difference of strength between recalled and forgotten items, even if there was also a difference in the availability of addresses for retrieval.

The result is not completely general: and everything I have said thus far applies to lists of forty items, with one list being given in a session. Under these conditions, however, people do behave in one way which is rather unusual. I mentioned earlier that in experiments on free recall the last few items presented are different from earlier ones. They have a better chance of being remembered. This is true, however, only with experienced subjects, who know that these items should be recalled first, before any attempt is made to recall the others. The reason for this is that earlier items will be remembered just as well even if you first spend time getting out the last items; but if you start with the earlier items, the last ones will have been forgotten before you reach the end and your total performance will therefore be worse. In terms of my standard analogy, perhaps the wise administrator should clear his In-Basket first thing in the morning before getting on with the long-term files. If he does not do so, as sure as fate somebody will come and dump another lot of stuff in the In-Basket on top of that which is there already.

However, this strategy of recalling the last items first did not appear in the computer experiments with only one list, and correspondingly the last items in the list were not particularly well recalled. We therefore tried a rather different arrangement in which six lists were given in each session, but only twenty items to a list. After each list, the efficiency of recognition was tested either for all items or for forgotten items. The first list of the session gave results like the previous experiment: that is, the last items were not recalled first, nor particularly well, and recognition was as good for the forgotten items as it was for the whole list. On later lists, however, the subjects began to catch on to the advantage of recalling the last items first, and they developed the pattern of superior performance on the last five or six items. At the same time, there began to be a discrepancy between recognition of forgotten items and of all items. I am still not sure what explains this change: presumably, it means that for practised people recall is dependent more upon the strength of an item, and rather less upon whether it has an available address for retrieval. This could be due either to a better and more efficient organization of addresses, or to changes in strengths due to the fact that, after the first few lists, one has many items of fairly high strength due to previous lists, previous recognition tests, and so on. Whatever the explanation, it is quite an interesting minor point from this experiment that the results you get are clearly associated with the strategy pursued by the subject, and I shall come back to this point. It does not affect the major point of these experiments, which is that in a substantial number of cases, forgetting has been shown to be due to some cause other than strength of the item as assessed by recognition.

I think I can fairly claim therefore that some function within the man finds one piece of information inside him rather than another, and uses this to determine his behaviour. As my last point, I want to illustrate the ways in which different schemes of addressing will give different patterns of behaviour. You will remember my own personal tendency, when looking for a scientific illustration, to pick an example of ideological conflict. This reveals, one might say, the titles of my mental files. But that example is very broad and crude: how can one refine the notion of systems of addressing? At this stage, we should turn to the use of different kinds of hint, to clarify the functional effects of using such methods.

Graham Hitch of Cambridge has set up an apparatus in which letters of the alphabet are presented to a subject in different spatial positions around him. Thus for example he might experience a series of letters, in which the first came from his left, the second from a little further to the right, the third further right still, and so on around the arc in front of him. His recall of an individual letter can then be probed in one of two ways: he can be shown the place where it appeared, or he can be given the item which immediately preceded it in time. As a third possibility, he can be given both kinds of hint simultaneously. This is yet another situation in which two hints are better than one, but in this case one can look rather analytically at the way in which this comes about. Errors of recall differ from one position to another, and this is particularly true for some kinds of error. You can distinguish errors which can hardly be due to retrieval, such as complete forgetting or recalling an item from outside the list. On the other hand, there is an important class of errors which consist of recalling an item from the wrong part of the list. You recall an item all right, but you have not found the correct one. These errors of retrieval are greater in the middle of the list: although the other kind of error is as likely to come from the end of the list as from the middle. (See also Fuchs 1969.)

Furthermore, the different kinds of hint give different patterns of error. Giving as a hint the spatial position of the desired item causes fewer retrieval errors than giving the preceding item; except for one very obvious exception, which is that a hint in the form of the preceding item never produces the preceding item itself as an error. When both kinds of hint are given simultaneously, each kind of error is reduced to the level of the better one taken alone. So each kind of hint excludes some possible errors, and having both kinds of hint excludes a wider variety than either kind of hint alone.

But one can look in closer detail at the way in which this happens. In the experiment thus far described, spatial position was perfectly correlated with time, so that the next item in time was always the next item to the right. Hitch has also tried the presentation of a sequence of items from positions which are uncorrelated with time of arrival. If now one gives a spatial probe to get recall of the particular item at that position, it is noticeable that the errors which appear are not particularly the items which came to right and left of that item. Rather they are the items which came before and after it in *time*. It seems likely therefore that the various spatial positions are remembered in a sequence in time, and also that the particular letters are recalled as a sequence in time, so that retrieval proceeds from a spatial position to the corresponding time in the sequence, and then from time in the sequence to a particular item. It does not proceed directly from spatial position to item.

Think yet again of the problem of filing my letters. I could organize a file by the topic with which they dealt, or a file arranged alphabetically by the person who wrote them. Or I could copy every letter and have both files, so that if I wanted the correspondence on a certain topic I could get it. But suppose that I wanted a letter on a certain topic, and the one that came out of the file was not only on a completely wrong topic but signed by the wrong person with a name similar to the one I wanted: so that the wrong letter has been retrieved because it was close to the correct letter. But as I started my search knowing the topic rather than the person, I must have had a list or index of the various topics, each accompanied by the name of the person who writes to me about it. Patterns of error are therefore extremely revealing of the system of filing which is being used. At least for this particular situation, it looks as if time is a more fundamental category than space in human short-term memory: but it may of course be quite different in long-term, and a good deal more exploration is needed in any case.

Some of Hitch's experiments also concern similarity in the sound of the name of the letter (B sounds similar to C, but not to R), and show that such similarity affects retrieval of an item given a spatial position, but not of a spatial position given an item.

Again there appears to be a systematic organization of features of an event, which makes retrieval asymmetrical. We can, therefore, come to the general conclusion that, when information is stored in human memory, some features are accessible through other features: just as, in filing correspondence, the individual letters are accessible through an alphabetical index, an index of topics, or some other partial description of the letter. Different methods of filing and retrieval are logically possible, and the kind which is used by any system, such as a human memory, will determine the ways in which it will perform well and those in which it will perform badly.

Let us think of a few different possible systems of retrieval, not in the case of human memory but of other processes. Think again of my correspondence. I could have organized it on a hierarchical system of classification, like the Dewey Decimal System in a library. That is, I could have had one drawer set aside for research grant applications, and within that drawer separate files for applications to the Medical Research Council, to the Social Science Research Council, to the Science Research Council, and so on. Within each of these files, I could have had a further sub-division, perhaps by taking the various people in the Medical Research Council Office, and keeping together the applications dealt with by each of them. In library systems this corresponds to dividing fiction from non-fiction, then within the latter separating science from the arts, then within science dividing physics from biology, and so on. Provided that one can fit one's material into a structure of this kind, it is extremely efficient at allowing rapid retrieval. For example, if I want to find grant applications handled by a certain man, I could find my way to them in the minimum of time. The trouble is that this is a system which only allows certain logical relations between the elements used for retrieval. It does not allow science ever to be fiction, or physics an art. That is why we sometimes cannot find a book in a library, because it has been put in a section which reflects part of the contents, but not the part which is attracting us to it.

There is another system which would overcome this difficulty.

This can be illustrated by supposing that I divide my grant applications into the different Research Councils, then within each Council alphabetically, and then within each alphabetical category place them in serial order of time of arrival. This carries a much smaller risk of mis-classification, because one is not faced with such terrible choices. It is perfectly possible for a letter both to be from the Medical Research Council, and also to have arrived on the 10 November: whereas in the previous system it would not have been possible for a letter both to be from the Science Research Council and also signed by Dr Chapman because he does not work for that Council. The trouble is that you end up with a fantastic number of files, and therefore getting to the right place is likely to take you rather longer, even though you may be more accurate when you get there.

In libraries this kind of system in fact often leads to special devices for retrieval, such as the following. If you have a set of index cards, each of them can be assigned to one possible feature of an item. If the cards were the index to a library, we could have a card for English History, a card for Sailing Ships, a card for Biographies, and on each card we would punch a hole whose position corresponds to a particular book. When, therefore, we want a book containing Biographies of historical English mariners, we would take the corresponding three cards and hold them up to the light. Where a hole appeared in all three cards in the same position, light would show through, and we would therefore be able to identify the particular books containing the properties we wanted. The more features we can use, the greater the probability of finding the book we want.

There are other possible systems as well, such as associative ones in which items possessing certain features refer us to other items having that same feature, these in turn refer us to yet more items which have features in common with the second set but not the first, and so on. If we think now of human memory, it is fairly certain that each of these systems will apply, and will do so at different times or in different people. The first system of hierarchical organization seems to be involved in the difference between the last five items experienced and memory for earlier ones. The use of combined retrieval cues, as in the cards with light shining through them, seems from the McLeod and Williams experiment to apply when several hints are given. The associative system is perhaps the most familiar of all, from the numerous work on repeated association. It becomes highly important therefore to know which of these systems is most used, what advantages each of them may have, and what the effects will therefore be on people who act using them. The difference between one method of retrieval and another is in many ways a more fundamental difference than that between somebody like myself who regards science as part of a general attitude to life, and on the other hand somebody who regards philosophy, politics, and science as completely separate categories. Both I and my antagonist might nevertheless both be using a hierarchical system of retrieval, and this might make us temperamentally rather the same kind of person: rather as it used to be observed that some people might be converted from Communism to Fascism, but never become social democrats. However, a person who thinks like the Dewey Decimal System may have great difficulty in understanding the processes of thought of somebody whose stored information about the past is organized primarily on the basis of an associative net.

I have been discussing systems of retrieval in terms of their abstract properties, such as whether they can only store items possessing certain logical combinations of features or not. I have also pointed out that each such system can be embodied in a library, in an office file, or in a computer as well as in the brain. This is the point to call up again an issue which I mentioned in the first Lecture, which you may have thought I had forgotten. I said at that time that the attempt to analyse human behaviour and to explain it scientifically had encountered three main kinds of objection. In terms of classic philosophical issues, these were the problems of purpose versus mechanism, problems of mind and matter, and problems of freedom and responsibility. I explained in the first Lecture the conceptual advances which have now

99

POINT LOMA COLLEGE
RYAN LIBRARY

stopped most people worrying much about the problem of purpose and mechanism. Since that time, I have said nothing about the other philosophical problems, but I had not forgotten them. Most of what I have said in the intervening four Lectures has been relevant to the second problem, the one I have labelled as 'mind and matter'. Although there are of course several different philosophical problems which might be so called, the particular problem I mean is the following.

People of good will have always felt that there was an important distinction between the way men thought, spoke, felt, and acted on the one hand, and the occurrence of isolated muscle twitches and nerve discharges on the other. The latter kind of event is clearly of the same kind as other physical happenings, while the former is of an importantly different kind. The scientific attempt to analyse behaviour was, I think, resisted at one time because it seemed to blur this distinction. Yet, from the scientific camp it seemed hard to find any way of describing behaviour except in physical and physiological terms.

Now, my previous four Lectures have all been a discussion of human function in terms which would as well be applied to any other system. That is why I have been able to use analogies like horse races, letter filing systems, servo-control loops, and other mechanical assemblies. In other words, I have been discussing information processing as a topic separate from the mechanical nature of the system which embodies it. We can have hierarchical classification in a library, office file, computer data structure, or in our own minds, and its logical properties remain the same in each case. Many different physical systems could have the same abstract functional description, and hence it is possible to discuss the function in abstraction from the gross physical events which embody it on some particular occasion. This is a form of discussion which has become widespread in psychology since about 1950, doubtless because in the same period it has become a matter of common experience that the functional analysis of a physical system can be separated from its material constituents. If we have two amplification systems, one made with transistors and the other with what you call tubes and I call valves, the two systems may differ in weight and in the ease with which they can be broken. But these are quite separate questions from the question of whether one of them has too much gain so that it will produce a howl when operating. Now, therefore, that all of us know numerous instances in which many different physical systems can serve the same function, we are used to separating function from structure. Since we are used to making this distinction within the physical world, it is entirely reasonable that it should continue to be made in the human case, and that one should distinguish the performance of the entire system from the particular physical events which happen to embody it. I do not think many people now are troubled by this particular problem, and it is just about disappearing from academic circles. Physiologists concerned with the brain would no longer feel it unscientific to make a functional or behavioural study as the first step to an analysis of the neural mechanism. On the philosophical side one can take as an example Fodor in his book on psychological explanation, where despite a generally traditional outlook he encounters no difficulty in accepting that a functional analysis may be a proper explanation in the absence of a physical one. He points out that, in an auto-mobile, a carburettor or a fuel injection system may serve the same function.

The theme of my middle four Lectures therefore has been the discussion of function in isolation from any physical or physio-logical basis. In this last Lecture, however, I have prepared the ground for my final step; because I have been discussing different ways in which filing systems, libraries, and so on could be or-ganized. In these cases, we are not simply dealing with different mechanisms which have a functional similarity, as in the case of a transistor amplifier and a tube amplifier. We are also considering cases where the same mechanism could serve different functions. You can have the same books and index cards, and two quite different kinds of index. This raises the point, which I have touched on already, that brains of the same general material basis can be organized in different ways. We have passed from the case of a common function expressed in different physical terms, to the case of different functions using the same physical elements.

Mechanical analogies for this distinction also now exist, but they have become widespread in experience only in the last ten years, with the spread of digital computers. I have just pointed out that the spread of thermostatic heating systems, servo-controls, hi-fi sets, and similar gadgetry, has familiarized us all with the existence of the same function in different physical forms. Although this has left some technical problems of the kind I have labelled 'mind and matter', it has caused most of us to stop worrying emotionally about them. The spread of computers has equally made some of us familiar with the idea that the same physical elements can be combined to perform different functions. My own feeling is that, as this distinction is gradually realized in common experience, the emotional difficulties about freedom and responsibility will disappear, even though no doubt there will remain technical and intellectual problems of interest. In the next and last Lecture, I shall be covering some of this ground.

6   Optimal Strategies of
Mental Organization

I want to start and finish this Lecture by quoting poems: because
a good deal of my message has to do with the difference between
scientific and artistic views of the world. I shall be arguing for the
scientific view; but only if we can preserve the advantages and
insights of the poetic one as well. Let me start then by quoting
Alan Bold, in a poem which describes how a constellation of
stars can look like a human figure. Bold goes on:

> I know I see like this because I use
> A heritage of seeing to direct
> All shapes into a schematic pattern.
> I know that man's great task is to unlearn
> These modes of seeing, that he must expect
> The unexpected. But what does he lose?

My answer would be that he *need* lose nothing of value; but
the question is a fair one. Applied to psychology, the question is
whether the analytic and behaviouristic attitude may lead to some
new form of tyranny, or at the very least to an impoverishment
of experience. If these dangers were real, they would be sound
arguments against experimental psychology. Even if we do save
lives by reducing airplane crashes, the quality of life is important
too. The case is similar to other earlier objections to behaviourism:
those who thought that a scientific account of man would
eliminate purpose or reduce mental processes to physical structure
were quite right to protest. The answers to these objections were

that purpose has to be included in a scientific account rather than ignored, and that function is different from structure because many structures can have the same function. But the traditional insights needed refinement rather than flat denial. The same is true of the concern which Bold and many others express.

As I said at the end of the previous Lecture, I think that the key difficulty here lies in the assumption that, although different structures can have the same function, yet the same structure cannot have different functions. This assumption is widespread, although quite false. It underlies the strategy of many experimental psychologists themselves, who devise experiments to find *the* way in which perception or learning occur; and of physiologists who look forward to explaining the psychologist's laws by finding the structure which underlies those laws. It is not surprising therefore that our critics think this assumption essential to the scientific enterprise; and then protest that in fact people do have freedom to vary their behaviour, and that they ought not to be treated in ways which deny that freedom.

The factual criticism is perfectly sound; there are now many experiments in which it has proved impossible to define the one way in which human beings perform a certain task. Rather, the psychologist can only list the various ways they may adopt, and show what advantages and disadvantages stem from each. Let me take three examples of increasing complexity.

First, take the case of visual search. Many experiments, particularly triggered by Dick Neisser of Cornell, have examined the problems of a man trying to find one particular object amongst the others; say, looking for his wife in a crowd (Neisser 1967). Broadly speaking, the usual conclusion is that different parts of the visual scene are examined successively, so that if the target is a particular word in a list of words, the time taken to find the target will increase if the target is further down the list. A similar problem occurs if you are using the London Underground and trying to locate the correct price of a ticket corresponding to your destination. There are various ways in which a list of stations can be presented, and in unpublished experiments of my own I found that people do not scan such lists in the way discussed by most theories of visual search. Since the list is in alphabetical order, people go directly to the approximate region of the station they want, and it takes no longer to find the price of a ticket to Wapping than it does to Hammersmith. Any account of visual search which regards successive examination of every item as a universal mode of functioning would be far too limited.

In that example, different methods of search are controlled by the nature of the situation. Sometimes, however, people treat even the same situation in different ways. Take a task which has recently been studied by John Morton in Cambridge. The man has to compare a patch of colour with the written name of a colour, and indicate whether they are the same or different. There are two conditions: in one case the name is written in a colour which is irrelevant to the task, while in the other case the name has to be compared with the colour of the ink used for writing another and quite irrelevant colour name. The question of interest is whether an irrelevant name is more interfering than an irrelevant colour; and Morton found that it was. But his results were in disagreement with some obtained by Anne Treisman of Oxford, and this was puzzling. It then emerged, from the introspections of a highly sophisticated subject, that there are two ways one can do such a task. You can look at the colour, name it, and then compare the names. Or you can look at the name, visualize the corresponding colour, and then compare the colours. If you are comparing names, an irrelevant name interferes; but if you are comparing colours the presence of an irrelevant name makes no difference. Some experimental subjects catch on to this fact by themselves and some do not; and you can instruct people to use one method or the other, and demonstrate consequent changes in their performance. The same task, the same brain, but two different and optional patterns of behaviour.

The third example is a little older, but gets closer to the optional strategies I particularly want to consider. It is due to Ralph Haber of Rochester, and it concerns perceptual selectivity or 'set'. Consider the task of looking at two cards and saying what is on them. Each card contains an abstract shape such as a triangle or square. The shape is printed in a colour, such as red or green, and it is repeated several times so that there is a number, a colour, and a shape associated with each card. When the two cards are exposed very briefly, the man may have difficulty in reporting all six items of information. If one tells him to report only the colours, he does better; but Douglas Lawrence of Stanford made the point that such an instruction can be just as beneficial *after* the cards have been shown as it is when given *before* the cards are displayed. That is, such an instruction seems to leave unaffected the actual intake of information, and merely to alter response. But this conflicted with other experiments using different techniques, which did seem to show that perception was selective (Lawrence and Coles 1954).

Haber's resolution of this discrepancy was achieved by distinguishing two ways in which people can perceive a pair of cards of the kind I have described. One way is to look at each card and list the various features on it, then going on to the other card. A man working this way would mutter to himself, 'Two green squares, one red circle' and it would not help him much to know in advance that the colours were the only features he should report. The other way of doing the task is to take each dimension in turn, and list the values present on that dimension. A man working this way would mutter to himself 'Two one, green red, squares circles': and it would help him to know in advance that colour was the dimension of importance because then he could take that feature first. People can be instructed to be Object Encoders or Dimension Encoders, and which way they work determines whether an experimental psychologist who studies them will get evidence favouring selectivity in perception or not (Haber 1966).

In each of these three examples, there are alternative sequences in which processes can occur, or alternative organizations of stored information which a man can use. In each case, one possibility is better and more efficient from some points of view, and another possibility is better from other points of view. To many of us, these problems will recall discussions from another field; the software problems of computers. A computer can be physically in perfect condition, and yet foul up your experiment, or your magazine subscription, or your charge account, for reasons which cannot be understood by looking at the engineering and trying to find faulty components. For those who have not been infuriated in this way, let me give a simple example.

A certain department store in Britain converted its accounting system to computer operation. For some months all went well; then one day without warning the output of the system became gibberish. There was nothing whatever wrong with the machinery and some time elapsed before the difficulty could be found. The explanation was this. Each day, the computer had up-dated the various charge accounts by entering the transactions of the previous day. It was of course necessary to remove from the memory accounts which had been closed, and to open new records for accounts which had been opened. Since it is often desirable to keep down the total demand on storage space in a computer, the arrangement had been adopted of starting by closing accounts and thus freeing some space which later could be earmarked for new accounts. What had happened to create disaster was that a lady had come in one morning and opened an account, but then over lunch had presumably discussed the matter with her husband, who took a different view. In the afternoon of the same day she came back to close the account. The computer had therefore found itself attempting to close an account when it had no record of that account having been opened, and when the corresponding region of storage was already occupied by something else. This had been enough to throw out the entire system. Such horrible examples are well known to computer people: absence of engineering faults is quite insufficient to guarantee that the machine will do what you want, because there may be some concealed trap in the sequence of operations or the method used for indexing and retrieving stored information. The same machine can operate in many ways, some of which work out properly while others do not.

During the last decade, this distinction between the problems of computer hardware and computer software has been borne in upon the consciousness of many of us, and has made it easy for us to see that the same brain could operate in many different ways. The problem of psychology is not therefore to describe the one unalterable set of principles which control behaviour, and which in due course will be explained physiologically. Our problem is rather to devise, elaborate, and compare many different possible ways of organizing the mind; an occupation which will never be replaced by physiology, just as in the case of computers software problems can never be answered merely by a perfect knowledge of hardware.

You will notice that I have used the informal term 'software', rather than referring in more formal style to the difficulties of 'programming' computers. The reason for this is that the formal word carries the wrong associations, because it goes back to the earlier era in which computers merely executed in a predictable sequence an invariant series of operations. In those days the machine would indeed do different things with different programs, but in each case the sequence was imposed by a series of input messages coming from outside the machine and determining absolutely what the computer would do. Applying *this* analogy to people, a believer in human freedom would hardly be consoled to hear that psychologists are concerned with the programming of human beings.

But the emotional over-tones of the word 'program' are no longer appropriate. In contemporary software systems, the computer is not confined to one string of actions; it may branch between various alternatives depending upon the results of its own calculations, upon fresh inputs, upon a combination of the two, or even upon the choice of a random number. It becomes, therefore, occasionally unpredictable even in principle, and normally unpredictable in practice. When the ordinary user of a machine attempts to get a job done, he may still speak of inserting a program, but his instructions are only interpreted or even accepted by courtesy of an executive program which was already in the machine when he approached it, and which has the power to decide what shall be done with any stimulus entering the sense-organs of the computer, including all too frequently ignoring it altogether.

Now, the psychological examples I gave earlier were chosen, amongst other reasons. to show exactly this kind of effect in the human case. In Haber's experiment on perceptual selection, a stimulus might be accepted by the man if he had himself chosen or had been instructed previously to use Dimensional Coding; and yet the same stimulus might be ineffective if the executive program was making use of Object Coding. In Morton's experiment, the stimuli were always accepted. What happened to them after that, however, was decided by a control process within the man, which might as you recall, translate a written word to a colour before comparing it to the presence of another colour; or alternatively translate a colour to a name before making the comparison. Thus there is a clear sense, verifiable in the laboratory, in which the majority of adult human beings are not at the mercy of some fixed schedule of instructions which might be fed to them by a dictator or a psychologist. They can reject altogether what is done to them, or they can accept it, examine it in the light of their own wisdom, and decide to act in such a way as to frustrate the purposes of the person who is trying to influence them.

Let us take the whole picture I have sketched of human nature in these Lectures, and see how much of the control of behaviour is internal. A man's movements are altered in detail by his environment and by momentary accident, but they are formed into actions by the command signal which launches each act, and which is part of the state of the man, not of the outside world. The command signal itself is not a sudden event, but the cumulation of a whole series of momentary impulses until a criterion is reached; and that criterion is set by the system itself and not by the incoming stimulus from the environment. The impulses to action come indeed from an earlier cumulation of evidence from the outside world, which produces perceptions. Yet those perceptions may never result in intentions, still less in actions, unless they are combined appropriately with signals arising internally. Further-more, the cumulation of evidence to give perception must again reach a criterion set by the man and not by the outside world: and the whole process is self-adjusting so that the particular sources of evidence used alter with the emotional state of the percipient. Last, but perhaps most of all, the impulses to action which arise internally, from the stored accumulation of past operations upon experience, are selected out of an enormous array of possibilities, and this selection is determined by the organization and indexing of the memory; which is a property of the man and not simply of the objective events which have happened to him.

If, therefore, behaviour is controlled from within rather than from without, what is the point of psychology and why does one need to condemn as immoral attempts to manipulate people? Realistically, one has to admit that the organized structure which controls a man's actions does not always do so perfectly. The system which selects sensory information can be led to take in certain stimuli by those who know its properties; as when, in reading the London *Times* recently, my eye was caught by a photograph of a naked lady, who turned out as I recall, to be advertising a company which sells pesticides and fertilizers. Since I happen to have no need for those products, I would not have looked at the advertisement if it had not used this technique; and I dislike the appearance in myself of behaviour which I have not intended. What worries many people about this kind of thing is, I suspect, not so much an unshakeable belief in free will, but rather a feeling that internal controls over action may be weakened if too many outside constraints are applied; and that responsi-bility for one's own actions is a delicate system which could possibly be put out of order by too much interference. My own guess would be that this is indeed true; that the particular prin-ciple of organization which emphasizes individual self-control is culturally determined and that cultures can exist in which it is less used than in ours. Nevertheless it seems to me a sound prin-ciple, on the same engineering grounds that make local closed-loop systems a better way of achieving some end than a system which makes no allowance for local conditions. (Have you ever lived in a building where the heating was controlled by one central thermostat, rather than different ones in different rooms?) If we do desire individual autonomy, then advertising, political brain-washing, or even the massive pressure to conform found in small communities, are all threats to it which do not need the aid of psychology to become serious. The knowledge which our subject can give is rather more likely to be a defence, by telling us the points at which we should guard ourselves, and the means of doing so.

Yet it might be regarded as wrong to attempt to influence the course of events in this way. R. D. Laing has expressed the view that badness or madness are merely forms of alienation which are out of step with the prevailing or statistically more common forms of alienation, which are regarded as sane. Such a view certainly makes it seem an inappropriate exercise of power for a psychiatrist to try to make his patients more normal. But Laing leaves aside a moral point here, that action does not necessarily correspond with intention; there are system failures in people just as there are in computers. As T. S. Eliot puts it,

> 'Between the idea
> And the reality
> Between the motion
> And the act
> Falls the Shadow.'

This experience of disharmony within one's own system goes back well before any psychologists were tampering with the mind. 'For the good that I would, I do not; but the evil that I would not, that I do' (Romans 7:19). All of us encounter it to some extent; but using contemporary techniques such as semantic differentials or repertory grids, we can put numerical estimates on the similarity or difference which a man sees between his own behaviour and that which he admires. Professor Gwynne Jones (1971), in his Presidential Address to the British Psychological Society, has cited clinical cases in which this has been done, which are characterized by very large discrepancies between self and ideal self. A recent study of U.S. Air Force men obtained correlations for each man between self and ideal self; a high proportion of those who were psychiatric cases actually gave negative correlations, whereas none of the control subjects did so.* This greater experience of lack of control over their own behaviour is exactly what brings people to the psychological services for help. Whether as yet they can get the help they need is another matter; but at least the effort to provide it is worth while. The difference between normal and abnormal is not in the direction which action takes, but in its success in achieving intention. Correspondingly, one can defend a moral distinction between political brain-washing and, for example, the use of conditioning techniques to cure a transvestite, just so far as the former is intended to reduce the individual's control over his behaviour and the latter to increase it by eliminating actions which the person himself rejects. At a different level, the improvement of aircraft instruments, the design of zip-codes which are easy to remember, or the linking of men and computers in ways which reduce error, are all examples of reducing the gap between intention and action.

To sum up, freedom is not a given and unalterable property of human nature which behaviourists are ignoring: it is an achievement which can only be reached with great difficulty, and with a detailed knowledge of the system on which it depends. Without that knowledge, the biasses imposed by our culture and by the limitations of our brains will control us, and it is one purpose of psychology to reveal these forces to us.

But if one does achieve self-mastery, what should one do with it? Can psychology offer any guidance? As yet, not much; but my hope is that it will be able to do so in the future. Just as an example, let me go back to the questions of organizing and retrieving stored information, which I discussed in the previous Lecture. You will remember that, if one is storing a number of

* See Bourne, P. G. (1969) (ed.) *The Psychology and Physiology of Stress with reference to special studies of the Viet Nam War*, New York: Academic Press. See also work by A. D. Ryle, to appear in *Brit. J. Psychiat.*

objects each having several properties, one may do so by structuring the whole system in several different ways. One could store together all objects having a certain property, then divide them again into separate sub-groups according to the presence or absence of some other property, and so on. Alternatively, one could list all the properties of each object and then find any desired object by some special retrieval system using combinations of properties. The first system is the more usual one in offices and libraries; it is quick and practical, but it does run the risk of missing some vital information if that particular item should be under the wrong heading. Notice that this distinction is very much like the one drawn by Haber in human beings, between Object Encoders and Dimension Encoders: one kind of person lists the different properties of an object, the other kind lists the different values for various objects of a single property. This kind of distinction does not just appear in tachistoscopic experiments. Gordon Pask of London has been studying recently the ways in which people learn an imaginary biological taxonomy, made up of animals supposed to be found on Mars (Pask 1971). A wide variety of information about these animals was made available to the subjects, and the sequence in which they examined it was recorded. They were also asked to explain the taxonomy subsequently to the experimenter. From these records there were a number of objective measurements which could be used to separate the people into two groups: Pask calls one group serialists and one group holists. Broadly speaking, the serialists consider a single feature at one time, and list the sub-species of animal which have it; whereas the holists consider the whole set of sub-species and for each of them consider the combination of features which that sub-species has. I cannot improve on quotation from the protocols to give you the flavour of the difference in type of mind.

'Zoologists have classified the Gandlemuller on the basis of physical characteristics. The three main types are Gandlers, Plongers, and Gandleplongers. Gandlers have no sprongs. Plongers have two sprongs. Gandleplongers have one sprong.

There are 4 sub-species of Gandler: M1, M2, B1, and B2. The Ms have one body, the Bs have two bodies. The M1 and B1 have a single cranial mound. The M2 and B2 have a double cranial mound . . . and so on.'

That of course was a serialist; now for a holist.

'I want to tell you about a funny Martian animal which has been recently discovered and classified by scientists conducting surveys. They are funny slug-like things with various protuberances. These animals are called Gandlemullers, because they churn about in the swamps near the Equator and Gandle is Martian for swampmud, hence swampmudmiller. (Muller is German for miller.) These things churn through the mud eating it by some curious process which means they eat and excrete at the same time. . . .' He goes on like this for about a page of protocol, full of their special sense organs for detecting the wingbeats of Owzards, and how if they haven't any sprongs they have to rely on camouflage for defence. Only then does he say 'There are 13 different sub-species, divided into three main types. There are four Gandlers, four Plongers, and Five Gandleplongers. You get these with various numbers of bodies, one two, or three, and a sub-species has a prefix M (Mono) B (Bi) T (Tri) to say which is which. There are two M-Gandlers, two B-Gandlers. Similarly there are two M-Plongers and two B-Plongers. Now in Gandleplongers you get the T-types. Oh, there are two sorts of Gandleplonger called alpha or omega depending on the sprong.'

If you have managed to hold out with me this long through these lectures, you probably found the serialists description of the taxonomy easier to understand than the holist one. There is no doubt that I have a serialist type of mind, which separates individual features of a situation one at a time, rather than preferring to have available all features simultaneously in their full richness. I would be driven crazy by an explanation which tells you about the derivation of Gandlemuller but doesn't mention that the absence of sprongs identifies an animal as a Gandler. But a serialist explanation is not better absolutely, only for serialists. Pask compiled two teaching-machine programs, one of which presented another taxonomy in serialist fashion, while the other presented it in a holist way. He divided his serialists into two groups, gave half the serialist program and half the holist one; and similarly with the other kind of person. Each group performed better on subsequent test if they had had a program appropriate for their own kind of mind. The incoming information was better stored if it was in a form appropriate to the system of indexing and classification which the particular man was employing. Each kind of person, I suspect, finds this hard to believe about the other: there is no intuitive understanding of what it is like to have a different kind of mind. The needs and preferences of the other person can only be approached through the neutral and public medium of his observed behaviour and of the concepts of information processing, logically connected to behaviour, which can describe both types of mind impartially.

Each method of organization has its own merits. Margaret Gregory and I have carried out a number of studies on perceptual selection, in which the man does better in some circumstances if he is selecting stimulus items which have some common feature; while under other circumstances he does better if he is selecting items marked by a combination of features no one of which is sufficient by itself (Broadbent 1970b). (The first strategy is the one I have long called *filtering*, while the other I label *pigeon-holing*. Broadly speaking, filtering is faster at discarding irrelevant material, and so is more useful when many unrelated things are happening around you; but it is more liable to intrusion errors. Pigeon-holing has the opposite qualities.) It seems clear that each mode of thought can be adopted voluntarily by most men, although by the time they are adults they have a preferred or habitual bias in one direction or the other. They may of course have started with such a bias in advance of experience; and it may also be connected with educational speciality. Liam Hudson carried out studies in Britain of boys who did relatively well at classical intelligence tests, that is, at choosing the one of several answers which possessed a feature indicated by the question. He compared such boys with others who did relatively well on so-called creativity tests, that is, at listing all possible uses (features) connected with a given object. The former were more likely to be studying science subjects, and the latter the humanities, although there were some interesting cases of disciplines such as the classical languages which blurred the border-line (Hudson 1966).

These points do not take us very far in telling us how to organize our minds; they are only hints and guesses, which lovers of T. S. Eliot will know should be followed by prayer, observance, discipline, thought, and action. But I can claim only that in relatively trivial cases we have sound evidence for optional strategies which people can apply to their own minds and which will make them better able to achieve certain purposes. Until this time, each of us has usually accepted some such strategies from our culture unconsciously. Of course we still have a long way to go before we have even finished learning the basic and unalterable principles of behaviour, the hardware limitations of the human computer. But we are already entering on the far more fruitful era, in which psychology will offer, not a glimpse of predictable and inexorable cog-wheels revoling in our heads, but rather an array of different possible modes of thought, which it will be in the power of each man to adopt or to decline depending on his purposes.

You will notice that I have been picking up in this lecture the various threads I left hanging in earlier ones, so as to complete the actions which I then commenced. There is just one large thread left, which provides the unity between the various parts of my own career. That is, the question of what is happening in this century. You will remember that I spoke earlier of my fascination with the seventeenth century, in fact with the period in which Harvard was founded. Many parallel changes occurred in society at that time; our forefathers saw them simply as a struggle for political liberty, whereas nowadays we emphasize more a shift of power from the landed aristocracy towards the smaller gentry and merchants, or bourgeoisie. This in turn was linked with a change in technical and economic possibility. Another side of the same complex of inter-related events was a shift in conceptual organization which made it possible to handle the new structure of society. One could almost describe this shift as a swing away from a predominantly holist mode of thought towards one which would use serialist methods in some appropriate cases. In the newer view, one could properly study the velocity and spatial displacement of the falling apple without considering its other properties, such as its relation to Adam and Eve; or one might sell goods to a man on the basis of cash without inquiring whether one was his liege man of heart and hand with obligations to think like him on every issue. One of the weaknesses of holist thought is that the same object may have conflicting properties, which the holist may have to deny or eliminate; the same man may be a satisfactory source of wagon-wheels and yet have a regrettable preference for a different form of prayer-book. Sickened with settling disputes by fighting battles the English founded the Royal Society with its motto 'Nullius in verba', and the development of the resulting intellectual framework has resulted in three centuries in which the two Cambridges could remain relatively stable. (Or even self-satisfied!)

Now, however, the limitations of the seventeenth-century synthesis are beginning to show. It had the characteristic that analytic, mechanical, serialist, or scientific modes of thought were applied outside oneself but not inside. Action originated within the personality, but took effect only upon the physical world, or perhaps upon other people considering them as devoid of will. At the philosophical level, the familiar line of thought is that of Descartes, descending through various idealist thinkers to a contemporary expression in Sartre; where the other person is seen as a threat to our own freedom because his actions are not predictable, and because we suspect that he in his turn looks upon us as objects. Such a mode of thought was all very well in the three centuries of expanding frontiers and of unanswerable force available to the exponents of these ideas. If your will met an obstacle, you either eliminated it, or moved on somewhere else. But in our time these two conditions have ceased to hold. The unrestrained exercise of will has reached a point where different wills are coming into conflict: at the economic level, the interdependence of different processes and systems has become such that the days of the independent bourgeois entrepreneur are numbered. Correspondingly, power is shifting again towards new sections of society. If this change is to be handled effectively, we need a new structuring of experience, comparable in scope to that of the seventeenth century. The need for it is foreshadowed in our ideological wars, as it was in their religious ones. They did not altogether know what they were doing, and I am quite sure that the same is true for us. But I will hazard a guess about the intellectual shape of things to come.

This time, the change in thinking will be towards the use of serialist thinking about ourselves and our consciousness, rather than leaving that domain purely to holism. Just as the seventeenth century took a conceptual step towards the control of nature, so now we are going to control ourselves more fully. This will mean treating our own modes of thought as being capable of alteration, just as our forefathers began to treat the English landscape, draining swamps, changing methods of cultivation, and creating the agricultural basis for the industrial revolution. The twentieth-century shift will also mean an increased awareness of other people's state of mind as being different from our own. Given massive economic interdependence, our own intentions can only be translated into action in the light of other people's intentions and needs, and we cannot judge those by examining our own consciousness. We shall need to become continuously aware that the perceptions, thoughts, and motives of others really are inaccessible by looking inside ourselves. Communication can be established only through the neutral ground of public events. I am saying in short that the application of scientific method to ourselves will be the intellectual change of this century, reflecting a new economic and social settlement just as the application of science to the external world reflected the settlement of the seventeenth century.

Such a change must provoke resistance, just as the earlier one did. A preference for old modes of thought would in this era take the form of continuing the distinction between viewing the outer world as mechanically dependent, and one's own will as autonomous and independent. Socially, such a view would favour a monolithic system in which conflicts are eliminated by the universal acceptance of a single will. This mode of thinking can of course be urged from different directions which take different views of the content which the triumphant will should contain: in chess, one can play the white side or the black side, and yet in both cases obey the same fundamental rules. The most conspicuous and unpleasant version of this kind of thinking was of course the Fascist movement, whose name has now degenerated into a mere term of abuse, with the unfortunate by-product that some of its doctrines are beginning to re-appear. Yet opponents of Fascism, such as Sartre, think according to the same fundamental mode of the inevitability of a clash between the assertion of one's own freedom and awareness of the needs and independent existence of others. A central character of his novel *Roads to Freedom* asserts himself in the end by the purposeless killing of oncoming Germans, the last refinement of free will. I do not think it accidental that the mind of Sartre was formed under German idealists, that is, in the part of European culture from which the Nazi movement emerged as a kind of weed. Nor is the publication of *L'Etre et Le Néant*, at a time and in a country dominated by Nazis and their collaborators, accidental. Of course, the white king does not share the guilt of the black king, but he does play on the same board.

If we are to throw away this particular chess-board, I feel myself that the Anglo-Saxon tradition, that of the two Cambridges, lies closer to the future than the existentialist one does: in the same way, though no further, that my hero Cromwell spoke more for the future than his opponents did. That is, a society in which the main cause of each man's actions lies within himself, in which he is in that sense free, can only be achieved if he retains awareness of other hypotheses and points of view;

if he appeals to outside empirical criteria rather than to his own intuitions to guide him in uncertainty; if he concerns himself with communication across cultural and personal barriers by basing his language on externally observable events; if he builds institutions which recognize plurality of morals, religion, and ethos. It seems to me a blind alley to assert oneself without reference to the will of others, and lines of thought which take self assertion as a starting point are fundamentally reactionary, even though like the Nazis they use the language of progressives. In the last resort it was this characteristic which my silent generation saw and rejected in Fascism.

Yet in the seventeenth century the Cavaliers did stand for something; for loyalty to persons, for beauty, for the intuitive insight. They had their truth too, and as T. S. Eliot says, they and their opponents are now 'enfolded in a single party'. We all ought to be holists in some cases and when it is appropriate. So as a good social democrat, I have tried throughout these lectures to understand what it is that our current reactionaries are trying to say; and perhaps to present it in such a way that serialists may see the point. It is right to uphold freedom. Yet a more scientific account of man will be a bulwark of that freedom, by revealing how the truths we take as obvious are merely the biasses induced by our culture, and by giving us a wider array of possible modes of thought. Let Eliot have the last word, in lines from his own meditation on the seventeenth century.

> 'We shall not cease from exploration
> And the end of all our exploring
> Will be to arrive where we started
> And know the place for the first time.'

Part II

SOME PARTICULAR ISSUES

The four remaining lectures were given on separate occasions, and each deals in more detail with one of the issues touched upon in Part I. The first concerns the issue of central control within the individual, and was a Presidential Address to the British Psychological Society in 1965. The second considers perceptual selection and the different possible systems of retrieval of stored information, and was an invited address to the American Educational Research Association in 1965. The third lecture was a Presidential Address to Section J (Psychology) of the British Association for the Advancement of Science in 1967: it considers the problems of thinking and problem-solving, as well as making a partisan plea for more psychology in Britain! The fourth was the Myers Lecture of the British Psychological Society in 1970: it outlines the great advances of modern linguistics, and indicates the point at which I believe conceptual advances in the description of language cease to be valid as theories of psychology. My thanks are due to each of the above bodies for permission to reprint the lectures.

One chronological thread is of interest; my gradually increasing disquiet from 1965 to 1970 over the claims made for linguistics as a psychological approach. During that time, the initial great contribution of the new concepts seemed to me to be weakened by a trend towards traditional mentalism. As some of the readers of the previous Lecture have felt that no linguist would make such claims as I described, I have added some specific references.

Perpetual Defence and the Engineering Psychologist

Some years ago I was involved in one of those experiments which would hardly be worth doing except that it required very little effort. It occurred to me that there might conceivably be a difference in speed with which word associations were given if the stimulus word was presented to the right ear as compared with the left ear. This seems an experiment with a very low probability of success, and consequently it was merely carried out in a very informal way using subjects who happened to be about the laboratory. As a matter of fact there was indeed some evidence in the results that there is a real difference between the two ears in this respect: but that is not the point which makes me think the experiment worth mentioning on this occasion.

One of the incidental results was that we relearned Marbe's Law, the one which says that a man who produces a word which is a very common association to a particular stimulus will do so faster than he will a word which is an uncommon association. This effect was so large that we had to pay quite a lot of attention to it, and we noticed, for example, that different experimental subjects differed quite widely in the number of common word associations which they produced. There was one member of the staff of the laboratory who never on any occasion produced a response word that had been produced by the majority of other subjects. There was also one member of the staff who always on every occasion produced the response word which the majority of his colleagues had also produced. Those familiar with the staff of the Applied Psychology Unit will require no prompting to learn that the latter person, who never under any circumstances said anything unusual or original, was myself.

To discover this about oneself is, of course, for middle-class people in Britain, rather disturbing. There have been current in the neighbourhood of Cambridge views that the truly creative and valuable academic person may well be of a divergent rather than a convergent frame of mind, and likely to produce large numbers of different uses for particular objects, uncommon word associations, and so on. I can of course produce some rationalized defences to the obvious implications of these views by recalling that the use of unusual word associations may perhaps be associated with less desirable qualities than creativity. To take just one example, Venables (1964) has confirmed that schizophrenics show a very high score on a measure of novelty of word association. Nevertheless, there is a certain smart in discovering that one says just what everybody else says; so in considering a topic for this address. I felt constrained to try and make it as different as possible from those of my predecessors.

I needed, therefore, a line of attack which should be unique; and I have decided that, whereas Presidential Addresses are usually reconciliations of the diverse points of view that may be found within the Society, I would attempt at least to be controversial and to be rude about every point of view in psychology except that which I advocate myself.

Having decided to do this I must take my stand as an engineering psychologist. There are those who suggest that, in describing oneself by the names of both these professions, one resembles the coloured gentleman who said that he should not arouse prejudice because of his colour, since in fact he was half Jewish. If there is a profession whose image is nearly as poor as that of psychology, it is that of the engineer. Naturally I cannot be expected to share this image. As far as I am concerned the necessity to make theories fit hard factual situations makes engineering a more demanding intellectual discipline than that of abstract science: and I believe, in fact, that most great scientific advances have originated in practical problems. Of course the economic importance of the practical problem may be no guide to its ultimate scientific importance, so that one should not let the practical gains from an investigation be one's criterion for pursuing it. Nevertheless, by looking at difficulties that arise in real life, one is forced to think more rigorously and to consider variables which it is easy to forget while in the fastnesses of theory.

I would like to start my main argument by saying that one such variable in psychology is the control which an animal or man exerts over the effects of the various treatments which the environment applies to him. The approach which has in its formal statements least emphasized this factor is perhaps that of Professor Skinner.

In selecting him as the first antagonist, one seems in fact to be following his own inclinations, since in certain writings he has himself singled out the supporters of information theory and cybernetics as the main modern opponents of his own point of view. In his book *Verbal Behaviour* he gives a sentence which indicates the divergence: he says 'the programme of a radical behaviourism left no originating control inside the skin' (Skinner 1957, p. 459). This sentence indeed, and its implications, seem at first sight unreasonable to those who use analogies from engineering to explain human behaviour.

If we take the analogy of a computer, even one of those of the present generation, it is certainly the case that the information which it receives at any time will be handled in quite different ways, depending upon a control residing within the machine. In simple terms, we may, for instance, be feeding the machine with a series of numbers representing the length and width of a large number of rooms in order to calculate the total amount of linoleum that is going to be needed to cover all the floors of them. As one number enters the machine, it may be placed in one area of store representing length, while the number which follows immediately afterwards will be placed in quite a different area of storage representing width. Before the next number is taken in by the receptors of the machine, the central control will take the contents of the two regions of storage, multiply them together, and add them to the existing contents of a third region of storage representing area. Only when it has done this may it take in the next number. What happens to any given input depends crucially upon the state of the central control. In the present generation of computers the machine may even be dealing with a number of different programs simultaneously, so that several different operators may unknown to each other all be feeding information into the same machine, which will decide for itself the sequence in which it will cope with the demands made upon it, according to rules which may involve a priority of importance as well as economic considerations of the time available. To the person who takes these large machines as analogies, the idea that control resides within the organism is certainly neither mystical nor unlikely.

Furthermore, there seems nowadays to be very adequate evidence that animal learning equally proceeds under control which resides within the animal. In recent years, one of the most striking illustrations has been the large body of experiments carried out by Professor Sutherland and Dr Mackintosh, mostly at Oxford. They have shown, for instance, that the differences between schedules of reinforcement, so dear to Professor Skinner, depend upon the previous history of the animal (Sutherland, Mackintosh and Wolfe 1965). Their plausible interpretation of this result is that an animal learning a discrimination takes in only certain parts of the scene in front of him, that one of his tasks in learning is to control efficiently his own input and that certain types of reinforcement teach him to ignore parts of his surroundings so that the effects of subsequent reinforcements are altered.

This is only part of a substantial body of work on observing or mediating responses, associated with names such as D. H. Lawrence, Wyckoff and so on. If you teach an animal to approach white shapes and avoid black ones, you are also teaching it to ignore shape, so that it will subsequently find it easier to do the opposite, to approach black and avoid white, than to learn some new discrimination of shape (e.g. Mackintosh 1962, 1965). In verbal learning by human beings a whole area of research is concerned with mediated transfer (e.g. Jakobovits and Lambert 1962). In that phenomenon, a previously established link between two words causes learning involving one of them to facilitate or impair learning involving the other. The work of Luria (1961 on the relationship between verbal and motor responses in children is of course well known, as is the Harvard work showing that the existence of colour names which correspond to certain parts of the visible spectrum affects the ability to learn fresh discriminations in the spectrum (Bruner 1957, p. 143).

There seems, therefore, to be a great deal of objective evidence for the importance of central control and mediating processes, which can only be left out of account in the programme of a radical behaviourism by using experimental situations such as Skinner boxes which eliminate those variables which are most important in the prediction of behaviour in most real life situations.

It might be thought that the recent successes claimed for behaviour therapy provide an argument against the primacy of language and of the organism's selection and control of the information which is reaching it. In cures achieved through conditioning, it would seem at first sight that the relevant associations are imposed upon a passive patient. Closer examination of case studies, however, reveals that this is not altogether true. If behaviour therapists are successful it is because they are too sophisticated to follow the example of Dr Brill, the eminent psychoanalytic pioneer in the United States, who tried to cure a patient of repeated belching by shouting 'shut up' loudly every time the patient belched (Brill 1944, p. 22). While such an approach may produce short-term benefit, it is on all points of view likely to show relapses. Without an analysis of the mediating responses (the stimuli which elicit the anxiety which the belching reduces or whatever it may be) one cannot on any theory expect to produce a permanent change in learning and therefore in behaviour. If one examines closely the procedure used by Wolpe and other successful practitioners of behaviour therapy, one sees that indeed the conditioning part of the procedure is preceded by a lengthy analysis of the situation in order to discover what particular method of attack is appropriate. In support of my belief that this is the case, I need only quote that well-known mystic and believer in psychotherapy, Professor H. J. Eysenck, who on page 157 of his new Pelican has a substantial passage emphasizing this point (Eysenck 1965): the key sentence is 'personal acquaintance with the people concerned leaves little doubt in my mind that Wolpe and some of the others concerned have a very special ability to understand the difficulties and troubles of the neurotic, and to devise ways and means of getting them out of those difficulties'. (If by any chance there is still some-body left in the Society who has not yet read this Pelican, may I attempt to attract them to it by the first clause of the next sentence, which Professor Eysenck starts by saying 'as one completely lacking in this ability'?) There is, therefore, no need to regard behaviour therapy as an exception to the general rule that the intake of information into a man or an animal is highly selective, and so indeed is its handling once it has been taken in.

In this way, then, as well as in some others, nervous systems are similar to man-made computers. But I have been most unfair to Skinner and it is necessary to look a little more closely at the precise way in which the internal control is established and located. In our example of the machine calculating an area of linoleum, before the series of measurements was fed to the computer, the machine had previously been programmed. That is, it had received a series of inputs which were placed in its storage, and which dictated the operations which it was about to perform and therefore what should happen to each successive number once the data was fed in. Skinner's terminology is not really inconsistent with this, since he wishes to argue that the apparent control by the organism itself, which we can see in many experiments, is actually the result of a past sequence of stimuli. Provided that one interprets Skinner in this sense, his statement is perfectly acceptable; but when we consider the analogy with the computer, we find that a prime concern in programming is to keep track of the part of the program which is in control at any instant, and the way in which control is passed from one part of the program to another. Similarly, it is not sufficient in psychology to trace back behaviour to the previous experience which provoked it; one must also consider the processes which led these stimuli rather than others to control present behaviour. In computers, a part of a program may remain completely ineffective if control is never passed to it, despite the fact that it has been received and is indeed in the store of the computer. For example, consider a program which is evaluating the average of a series of input numbers until that average becomes greater than X or less than Y. The cycle of operations of reading a number, working out an average, and comparing it with X and Y, will continue until one or other of the limits is exceeded. When that happens, the program will instruct the computer to go to a fresh part of its own storage and receive instructions about its next step. If, in fact, the average has become bigger than X, then it may be store A that is consulted, while if the average is less than Y, it may be store B that is consulted. If control passes to one of these stores, the other may never become effective at all. Indeed, at this stage, I can advance my general argument a further step. I have said, firstly, that in machines a central control selects the course of action to be followed; secondly, that similar controls apply in men and animals, and now thirdly, that the handing of control from one place to another is carried out by means of the address in the store which is to be consulted next. If an address is not used, or is for some reason unavailable, the information in that part of the store will not show itself in the output of the computer.

A concrete example of a programming failure was given in Lecture 6 of Part I. Anybody concerned with programming will find such difficulties familiar enough and perhaps rather trivial. Those who have not encountered this sort of situation, however, should realize that the programming of a computer is quite a separate problem from its physical reliability and that a complete understanding of its mechanism is not sufficient to cure most of its operating faults. This, of course, is an opportunity to take a swipe at physiological psychology before continuing with my general argument. You would not understand what was going on in the computer by tracing its wiring diagram and a knowledge of physiology is to the same extent necessary but not sufficient for an understanding of behaviour.

Control passes about the computer then by means of addresses in the storage system. The older generations of machines were programmed in an arbitrary code, which had to be learned by the humans who produced the original program. In such cases the address in storage would be indicated by some reference peculiar to the machine. Equally no doubt in animals and to quite an extent in man the key events which transfer control occur in some code private to the particular individual. More recently, however, there have been developed conventional languages so that one can write a program which can later be used on any one of a number of machines. These programming languages have their own rules or grammar, and the procedure is that the computer is first given one series of inputs which tell it how to translate into its own private code the next series of inputs, which obey the conventions of the particular language concerned. The first group of inputs, which tells the machine how to translate, is called the compiler, or sometimes one of other rather similar terms. Obviously, once one expert has written a compiler, anybody else who knows the general language can use the particular machine by borrowing the compiler and writing programs in the language that he knows.

At this stage I might point out certain similarities which seem to develop between the language of those who are concerned with programming problems and the language of some people dealing with human problems. Thus it may be asserted that a particular phrase is inserted in the program in order to indicate 'to the compiler' that such and such is the case; or it may be said that the compiler takes no notice of information of a certain type. It would seem that programmers, like early Freudians but unlike Skinner, think of the series of previous stimuli as being in some way embodied in a little man within the computer, or at least to find it convenient to talk as if they did.

One of the features of these languages is that certain parts of the storage of the computer are represented by names which the programmer can make up for himself. Thus in the language known as ALGOL one may start out the program by listing a series of names which one proposes to use during the program, and when they are 'declared' in this way, the computer allots part of its storage to each of the names concerned. Thus in an example similar to that I have already used, one might say that one was going to use the names length, width and area, and the computer would allot three regions of storage to these three names. Having announced that one was going to use these names, one could then make a series of statements such as:

length: = read
width: = read
  area: = length × width

This would tell the computer to read the next input number into the 'length' store, the one after that into the 'width' store, and then to extract the contents of both stores, multiplying them together, and put them in the store reserved for 'area'.

Now at this stage let us draw a tempting analogy. The basic instruction to a computer consists of an address in storage and an operation which is to be performed using that address. The basic grammatical distinction in English is between the noun phrase and the verb phrase in the sentence, namely between a part of the sentence which names something and a part of the sentence which tells us something about it. The tempting analogy therefore is that the noun phrase, the name, corresponds to an address in storage while the verb phrase, the 'telling' part of the sentence, corresponds to an operation that is to be performed at that address. The idea is that when we say to a person 'John is 16' he is like a computer which has a part of its storage labelled 'John' and which inserts into that region of its storage the information '16'. To go a little further, it is of course perfectly possible for the verb phrase itself to contain words which can on other occasions act as noun phrases, just as in the computer part of the contents of one store may be the address of another part of store to which control is next to pass. So when we say 'John is the brother of Jane', we are storing under the label 'John' instructions which will refer us to the store labelled 'Jane' next time we encounter 'John'.

Let me recapitulate. Central control selects the input and the way in which input is processed, both in computer and in man. This control passes from one area of memory to another by means of addresses which may be purely private events. But in computers they may also be public events, words, which can play a similar role in many machines; and here we have an analogy for the part played by language in human beings.

Before I go on to my last and main point, which of course concerns perceptual defence, let me describe a minor experiment to support the view I have been putting. In ALGOL, a name must be declared before it can be used; in FORTRAN, another language, one can introduce names of certain types as they are needed without preliminary declaration. They are recognized for what they are by the compiler and appropriate storage is allotted; but even in FORTRAN one needs to declare the name of, say, a function rather than a simple variable. Human language goes a step further and we can to some extent pick up what an unknown word means by observing its usage without having a strict preliminary definition. Some of the conventions used are extremely subtle: I can recall reading a children's story to my young daughter which commenced as follows: '" Let's go for a picnic," said Mummy to John and Jane. The twins were delighted.' It may have been too much Christmas dinner, but I wondered for some time who these twins were.

But now consider somebody listening to a series of statements about the structure of a family. He might hear: John Smith is a friend of mine. Mary is John's wife. Richard is Mary's son. Alice is Richard's wife. Ted is Alice's father. Jane is Ted's wife. Such a series of statements is perhaps reaching the limits of memory on one presentation, but is not completely hopeless. Imagine, however, what would happen if the same series of statements were delivered in a different order. Instead of each new name being introduced by its relationship to an existing person, each statement would contain two new names to be placed in relationship to one another. Mrs Gregory and I have, in fact, constructed family systems in this way, made up of six statements, which can be delivered in two orders. In one order the verb phrase of each sentence contains a noun that has been used in the noun phrase of the preceding sentence and by analogy with the programming

TABLE I   The first four statements of a family in chained order

Noun Phrase	Verb Phrase
John Smith	is my friend
Jean	is John Smith's daughter
Bill	is Jean's husband
Oliver	is Bill's brother

language can be regarded as a declared variable. In the other order, at least the first three sentences have no name in common. Two sequences of sentences were presented, one in each order, to each of eighteen people. It was found that reproduction of the content of the sentences was significantly better when the sentences followed what one can perhaps term the rational order. Thus it does appear that there is an analogy between the difficulties which may appear in programming a computer and those which may arise in delivering a series of statements to a human being for understanding. It may be possible that this result can be handled by classical theories of verbal learning, but it is certainly not obvious. This is perhaps because the functionalist approach to verbal learning of, for example, Postman or Underwood, despite the massive contributions which it has made, is dominated by a theoretical preconception that association between input and output is the key factor in learning. The analogy with engineering devices at least makes it evident that there are other possibilities.

We have carried out a similar experiment using sentences which make up a continuous story rather than a family structure, and the results are the same.

TABLE 2 The first four statements of a story in muddled order

Noun Phrase	Verb Phrase
The noise	was inaudible to the office manager
The strike	was caused by the electric typewriter
The youngest girl	worked away from the other secretaries
The duplicating machine	made a good deal of noise

TABLE 3 Statements correctly recalled (maximum 6)

	Presentation		
	Chained	Muddled	P
Families (one presentation)	1·75	1·042	<0·05
Stories (two presentations)	5·46	4·64	<0·025

If people hear six sentences describing an industrial dispute in one order, they receive all the information but cannot remember it; the style seems difficult and obscure. Present the sentences in another order so that each name is declared before it is used, and the story becomes easy to remember. This kind of approach to language does provide a way of making clear the difficulties which some of us have in handling the psychological statements made by some of our colleagues. I may take as an example a recent textbook of psychotherapy, which it would be invidious to name since it is in many ways excellent. Nevertheless, the style in which it is written presents the same kind of difficulty to the reader as did our family structures when we presented the sentences in random order. The novice reader is introduced to psychotherapy through the concept of 'object need'. This term is explained as equivalent to 'primal transference', and by saying that everybody has a definite need for 'real objects', independent of any 'specific neurotic structure' or of 'infantile projection'. The patient and the therapist share this need, but nevertheless establish a 'therapeutic relationship'. This takes place because the therapist interposes a 'barrier to reality'.

At this stage in this introductory textbook, the reader has labelled a large number of regions in his storage with words that will enable him to find them again: but he has not as yet received information to put in those areas of storage, which may perhaps lead him on from one area to another. In fact the meaning gradually emerges during the succeeding chapter or so, but comprehension for the inquiring novice is made difficult by the use of terms which are given content only through their relationship to one another, rather than through any explicit definition. This kind of error of style is not of course confined to the psychodynamic point of view, although it does seem to me to be rather frequent amongst upholders of that view.

Much of what I have said is consistent with many older approaches. The conception that the name of an object or of an action is important, because it allows us to find the relevant information about that object or action in our memories, can with some effort be translated into the language of mediating responses, or to yet more traditional ideas. Attention has often been drawn to the magical importance which is attached in many primitive societies to knowledge of the name of another person or of a god. Remember, if the name is unavailable, the necessary information may be in memory but is effectively useless. So my general line of argument has justified us in showing great interest in the extent to which particular words are available to a man: because those words may represent in a public form the way in which the central control of behaviour is handled.

One way in which a name can become unavailable is, as we have just seen, by an error of programming. Another way in which naming can be disordered is through damage to the brain, and in this connection the recent studies of the Psycholinguistics Unit in Oxford have been of great importance (Oldfield and Wingfield 1964).

One of the important ways, however, in which a name may become unavailable in human beings is simply that the input information is not recognized as an instance of the class of cases to which it is appropriate to apply this name. C. S. Lewis, you will remember, made his senior devil counsel a young tempter not to allow the human being under his charge to apply the term 'anger' to his own state of mind on hearing an insult, lest he should take the appropriate action to control himself. It may indeed make all the difference to the later reactions that occur in a situation if one has or has not applied the correct name to the situation. Thus by studying the availability of names, one may hope to shed some light on the clinical problems which arise when somebody does not describe his own motives and actions in the terms which seem obvious to an outsider. There is little doubt that some names are easier to apply correctly than others are. You will be familiar with the long controversy that has raged about the perception of obscene words, under the general title of perceptual defence. Much of this argument has concerned the question whether the peculiar difficulty in hearing an obscene word is due to its emotional quality, or simply to the low probability that such a word would be used by an eminent professor as part of a psychological experiment. This particular argument I do not propose to discuss in detail, because nobody disputes the fact that the perception of a word would depend very much indeed upon its probability of occurrence: but this itself requires explanation. Why is it easier to perceive a word which is probable than a word which is improbable?

At this stage in my address I feel that I should consider the situation to see if there is any class of psychologists who have not as yet been sufficiently abused. We seem to have covered enthusiasts for operant conditioning, physiological psychologists, psychodynamic authors, behaviour therapists, verbal learning functionalists, and a few miscellaneous groups such as enthusiasts for creativity. In order to complete the score perhaps we should cite a certain theory of perceptual defence which appeared in 1958, and which was moderately in accordance with some of the views I have already expressed. According to this theory the organism could select certain channels of incoming information, and possibly therefore was set to reject the stimuli appropriate to certain classes of words, such as obscene or, we may presume, improbable words. The process was regarded as analogous to the rejection of information reaching the eyes when one is concentrating on listening, or the rejection of information at the ears when one is reading. This remarkable naïve view, contained in a book called *Perception and Communication* (Broadbent 1958), came heavily under fire in the course of the next few years from investigations carried out in Oxford. Not only was it shown by Moray that the threshold for words was no lower when the listener was required merely to identify which class they belonged to than which word they were (Moray 1961): but even more severe difficulties were raised by Mrs Anne Treisman, who has in 1965 become the first Spearman Medallist of this Society. Perhaps the most basic of Mrs Treisman's experiments was one in which she showed that a listener who was attending to words arriving at one ear, while ignoring words reaching the other ear, might nevertheless perceive an occasional word which stimulated the wrong ear but which was highly probable in the context of the words which had been perceived on the ear receiving attention (Treisman 1960). This and other important investigations made it clear that attention does not simply switch off some sense organs and leave others switched on: and suggested to Mrs Treisman a kind of double theory of attention, according to which the incoming information from the senses serves to select the most appropriate unit from a kind of dictionary contained within the brain. Information from some senses may be given more weight, so that one does indeed neglect information from one's ears when one is reading as I myself had suggested; but in addition some units within the dictionary, some categories of response if you prefer, are unduly biassed towards occurring. The reasons for this bias might be probabilistic (because of context), or emotional, but the actual mechanism by which they produce their effect would be the same in either case.

Let me summarize my argument thus far. First, there is a central control within the man or animal which must be taken into account in predicting the effects of any particular stimulus arriving at the senses. Second, this control may be exercised through particular symbolic events which serve to set the whole system on one path or on another. In a computer these may be the labels of the names by which control is passed from one part of a programme to another: in the human case they may well be the names or other units that occur in language. On Mrs Treisman's theory some names are more likely to be used than others, regardless of the source of information which is entering the system. The next step, therefore, is to find out how these names are applied to particular configurations of outside stimulation: and for this purpose an extremely useful tool for investigation is the effect of word frequency. Thanks to those intrepid investigators who have counted the number of occasions on which individual words occur in passages of English, we do know reasonably well which words are probable in the language as a whole and which are not, and we also know that the probable words are more likely to be heard correctly in noise than the improbable ones. Furthermore, we know that this does not apply if we use a small fixed vocabulary of words and tell the listener which words are in the list, so that we are reasonably sure that it is not due to some feature of the acoustics of the words themselves: it is something in the adjustment of the listener to the probabilities, and it disappears when he has a fixed list and assumes that all the words are equally likely. How then does probability affect the perception of words?

There are basically four theories current in the literature, although they do not seem to have been very carefully distinguished from one another. First, there is the theory that words are perceived correctly on a certain proportion of the occasions when they are presented; and then, on a proportion of the remaining occasions, a perceptual event occurs which is not in fact determined by the stimulus but rather by guessing. Occasionally, this essentially random perception will, by chance, be correct, and if the guesses are of probable rather than improbable words, the apparent score will be better for probable words. This is the theory based on the traditional guessing correction, so long familiar from courses on psychometrics and psychophysics.

Second, there is a more sophisticated view, according to which the information from the senses rules out a number of possible words but leaves certain possibilities still appropriate. The perceptual event, when it occurs, corresponds to one of these, but the stimulus plays no part in deciding which one occurs. Rather, there is a preference for words which are more probable at the expense of those which are less probable.

Both these views assume that words are perceived, names applied in the more general case, through two separate processes of accurate perception and of essentially autonomous guessing, combining so as to give more frequent perception of the more probable alternative. It will be clear that both theories predict that errors will be more likely to be common words than uncommon words, and if a suitable allowance is made for the fact that there are fewer common words in the language than uncommon ones, this is indeed the case. While this is not the place in which to develop the mathematics, however, both these theories also predict that the ratio of common to uncommon words amongst errors should be lower when the stimulus is actually a common word than when it is an uncommon word. As we shall see, this is not the case at all, and consequently both these theories, which seem to be quite widely held, are completely inconsistent with the facts.

The third theory is the one put forward in *Perception and Communication*, that the sense-organs relevant to certain words are favoured. One could derive this kind of approach from the fashionable motor theory of speech perception put forward by Haskins and M.I.T. workers (Liberman *et al.* 1963). On this view, the listener attempts to articulate the incoming sound, corrects his attempt from the discrepancy between it and the input, and so finally attains correct perception. If the attempted articulation were of common words first and uncommon words later, the correct perception of the common words would be easier. On the other hand any difference between the actual stimulus and a common word should also be easily detected. Whichever form of this theory one tests, and again skipping the mathematics, it predicts that, if we take the ratio of correctly perceived words to perceptions which are wrong but are of the correct frequency class, this ratio will be greater for common than for uncommon stimuli.

The last theory is based on statistical decision theory, which, of course, I have to get in somewhere. On this view the senses provide evidence about the nature of the word which has been presented, and this evidence is no more accurate when a common word has been presented than when an uncommon one has; and no less accurate for an obscene than for a decent word. The listener, however, has a prior probability of hearing one word or another, and in the light of this he sets his criterion so as to demand more convincing evidence for an improbable word and less convincing evidence for a probable one. This means, of course, that his incorrect perceptions will be probable words, although he is not guessing at random. Rather he is behaving like a psychologist who accepts a result significant only by a one-tailed test provided it confirms the previous hypothesis.

On this last view, correctly perceived words will be a constant fraction of those perceptions which are wrong but of the same frequency class as the stimulus. So by doing an experiment on the perception of words, and making up a table of the number of errors which are common and uncommon words separately for common and uncommon stimuli, one can distinguish between these four theories. Mrs Gregory and I have done this, and our results are consistent only with the last theory: given a rather murky stimulus, the brain will accept a one-tailed test if the result favours a probable word, but demands a higher level for an improbable word. Our results are also consistent with those of earlier workers such as Brown and Rubenstein (1961), who have disproved the first three theories without explicitly testing the last one.

Although we have been working purely upon the perception of probable and improbable words, the same mechanism should explain also the failure to perceive or use words which have been punished when used inappropriately. Experiments on the detection of meaningless sounds, carried out in Michigan and many other centres, have shown that a man demands a stiffer criterion for detection if he is fined 5 cents for every false detection and gains only one for correct perceptions rather than gaining five for correct detections and losing one for incorrect (Swets 1964). It seems to me, therefore, that experimental and engineering psychologists have demonstrated a mechanism which will raise and lower the probability that a man will apply the correct word to some situation; and, as I have argued earlier, if he uses the wrong word this will affect the central control of behaviour and so produce widespread consequences.

Does such a mechanism have clinical implications? I think it does. This mechanism attributes failure to use a certain word to a *prior* setting of the criterion for that word, and not to the actual evidence coming up for decision. To put it in other terms, if it is found that a patient resists some interpretation of his behaviour, this is not to be regarded as evidence of the truth of that interpretation, but rather of a certain rigidity of conceptual structure which might be obscuring some other and quite different difficulty. I will not, however, pursue this hare too far, as the gamekeepers are doubtless already cleaning their shotguns. I merely wish to urge that the techniques of mathematical psychology and of psycholinguistics must in the end be applied if psychological medicine is to follow the course of physical medicine from herbal remedies to antibiotics.

To go back to my starting point any such development will no doubt have just as serious an effect on experimental psychologists as it will on clinical ones. We are, in fact, studying one subject, not many, and the proof is that I have failed in my attempt to shoot down competing approaches to my own. I have been forced to use data from Skinnerian animal workers, from verbal learning functionalists, behaviour therapists, and so on, in order to fit my own line of work into any recognizable general account of behaviour. We cannot, in fact, do without each other; and if the particular synthesis that I have attempted is not true, then something much more interesting is. I am glad, therefore, that there is little danger of this Society forgetting that, although the President speaks from the Chair, he does not therefore speak *ex cathedra*.

The Well Ordered Mind

At the beginning of George Eliot's great novel *Middlemarch*, the heroine's uncle inquires how one of his friends arranges his documents, and is told 'in pigeon holes'. 'Ah,' says the uncle, 'Pigeon holes will not do. I have tried pigeon holes, but everything gets mixed in pigeon holes: I never know whether a paper is in A or Z.' 'I wish you would let me sort your papers for you, Uncle,' said Dorothea, 'I would letter them all and then make a list of subjects under each letter.' Many of us who have to deal with a fair number of written documents are only too thankful if we have somebody like Dorothea to bring some system and method into the task, not merely of keeping and preserving the documents, but of finding the one we want on the occasion when we want it. It is a matter of harsh everyday experience that one need not worry very much about losing things in the sense of destroying them accidentally or sending them off to some other person; what you really have to worry about is being able to find them without going to every document on your desk and every file in the cabinet.

This difficulty is inherent in the whole idea of storing information for later use. But we ourselves are equally systems which store information for later use, just as the files in our office or the libraries of our academic institutions are. It seems likely therefore that our own nervous systems must encounter problems closely similar to those which appear in files or libraries. Indeed, I was interested to note that, in a hearing before a sub-committee of the United States Senate on 8 June last year, a distinguished Senator from North Carolina remarked that he did not confess to his constituents who see his desk that his mind is in the same disordered condition as his desk. The record showed laughter at this point but those of us who, like myself, do not altogether adhere to the principle of the clean desk, may experience some unease at the analogy, and may regard it as far too threatening and serious a matter for laughter. Consequently, when I was asked if I could give this talk on this occasion, it occurred to me that there might be some others with consciences as guilty as my own, who might conceivably welcome the opportunity to think about the organization and operation of memory. One slight snag in this intention is that I rapidly realized that I could provide little information as to the best way of achieving the well ordered mind: but then it is such a blessing to the man who fails to recall names or references, or to remember how to differentiate the product of two quantities, if the sufferer can only realize that other people are in just the same mess as he is himself. Furthermore, there are nowadays a number of lines of attack on the problems of retrieval which might conceivably shed some light on human memory, so that even if there are no answers, there may at least be a profitable language in which to ask the questions. In what follows, therefore, I am going to raise queries about memory, and toss them about a bit, but hardly, I fear, answer them.

Perhaps the most obvious naïve view of memory with which many of us started our lives, before we became interested in education or psychology, is that it is simply a record within the brain of the series of events which have occurred to a man during his life, laid down in the order in which they happen. When at some future date I wish to know what happened at some time in the past, I consult the appropriate portion of this record. Of course, even the most naïve view of memory will rapidly recognize that the record is highly selective, so that some things are never even noticed at the time they happen, and consequently do not get stored away in memory. It is also true that some things which are noticed and which produce a reaction, may not be recorded in memory; the record of a particular episode may consist only of a few key items together with a knowledge of the probable structure of all such episodes, so that one remembers to a large extent what is probable. Sound as these principles are they do not by themselves alter the naïve picture of the cinematograph film or the magnetic tape storing a sequence of experiences: they merely tell one more about the form of the storage.

If, however, we consider a relatively orthodox academic library, we can see that the chronological storage of the incoming information is by no means the whole story. Usually the books do tend to be added to shelves in the order in which they are published. This may be particularly true of one's own domestic library: it saves a lot of work rearranging all one's books just because a new one has come into the house. However, the usual technique in any substantial library is rather to keep a number of separate storage places, each of which accumulates books in the order of publishing, but each of which is devoted to a certain class of books. A widely used criterion of division is the subject matter of the book, so that one may find that part of the library is devoted to the sciences, and another to the arts, that within the sciences there is a distinction between physical and biological, and so on. The well-known Dewey Decimal System of classification is a method of this kind. It depends upon a series of successive sub-divisions, and once one has entered one particular sub-division, one cannot get across to other books outside it. For example, in the Cambridge University Library, within the shelves devoted to psychology, large psychological books accumulate for convenience on different shelves from small psychological books. The same distinction is made within other subjects. It is not, however, possible to find any single shelf on which all large books, regardless of subject matter, are being placed. That perhaps is of little moment, but it is more serious that the inquirer for a book does not usually arrive at the library armed with the date at which the book entered the library and with its subject matter, but rather knows other information about it which has not been used in placing it on a particular shelf. For example, he knows the name of the author and the title of the book. There is therefore in the library another record, which does not contain the books themselves, but rather consists merely of authors and titles, arranged in an order which is quite different from that of the books. If you look up the author and find the right book in this index, you get the address which refers you to the right place on the right shelf where you can find the book itself. If I may labour just one last obvious point about libraries, the existence of this index shows that each book, when it arrived, has been examined by a librarian. Not only has he put it in a geographically quite separate storage which depends on the subject of the book and therefore its content, but also he has extracted some of the information about the book and put it in the index.

All these points are very familiar and obvious, although I'm afraid we all take them rather for granted if we are not professional librarians. I emphasize them, however, because each of us is in many ways meeting a problem like that of a library: he receives a long stream of incoming information from his senses, from birth to death. He encounters problems at one time which can be solved by reference to earlier information, and he therefore has to extract this earlier information. In the case of libraries, however, it does not appear to be very useful simply to arrange the incoming information in order of arrival, and it is not sufficient even to divide it up into a number of separate stores each of which then is separately arranged in order of arrival. With such a system, if one receives a query for some information without knowing the exact date or time at which it was received, one must scan the whole of the relevant store. You might feel that this process could be made tolerable by a sufficiently fine sub-division of subject matter, so that there were only a few items in each of the ultimate stores. In that case, however, there is a very high probability that the item was put on its arrival in a store other than the one one now thinks appropriate. Consequently it does seem essential, for efficient retrieval, to maintain a quite separate storage system organized in a different way, which allows one to select the right item from memory from amongst all the other irrelevant items. This is indeed a truism of contemporary retrieval system theory: yet in the analysis of human memory relatively little attention is paid to the intermediate file or index which might be supposed necessary if selection of the right item from memory is to be easily possible. If our memories are like the gradually increasing rows of books on the shelves of a library, then what corresponds to the index?

At this stage, let me heave a sigh of relief, and turn from these rather general considerations towards experiments. One of the most influential papers recently advocating the analogy between human recall and the search of some non-human store of information is one by Yntema and Trask, published three years ago (Yntema and Trask 1963). They were concerned with an experiment in which the person being studied wore earphones, with each ear receiving quite separate information. He was given a whole list of items, say half a dozen, with half the items arriving at one ear and the other half simultaneously at the other ear. He was then asked to reproduce all the items. I should perhaps explain that this general type of experiment had been launched about twelve years ago by myself: in the version I used originally, all the items the man had to remember were digits (Broadbent 1954). He might receive, say, 723 on one ear and 645 simultaneously on the other ear and he had to remember them all. He tends to find this very difficult, unless he hits on the idea of reproducing everything from one ear first, and then going over to the other ear and giving you what reached that ear. If you make him try to produce the digits in some other order, he does badly.

Now I had interpreted this result as being due to something which had nothing whatever to do with the problem of retrieval which we are discussing today. I had rather argued that the phenomenon was due to the similar but distinct problem of dealing with all the information that is striking one's senses at any one moment. There is so much information that the nervous system is almost obliged to hit on various techniques for economizing its efforts, and one of these I suggested was to analyse only those patterns of stimulation striking some of the senses at one time. Thus two spoken digits, one on each ear, were too much to be dealt with simultaneously, and the brain had to select only the information coming in through one ear if it was not to be overloaded in its task. This selection, I felt, would take time to change and it was therefore easier simply to select all the information from one ear, and then afterwards to collect the other information from some kind of buffer or temporary storage attached to the other ear.

Now, there are a large number of other ways in which one can do this experiment. The particular modification with which Yntema and Trask were concerned was one in which you do not use six items belonging to the same general class, such as digits, but rather have some items belonging to one class and other items to another class. For example, you can have three digits and three letters of the alphabet, or three digits and three colour names. If you mix up the two classes of items on the two ears, so that each ear receives two items of one type and one item of the other type, then it is no harder to reproduce the three letters first and then the three digits, or the three digits first and then the three letters, than it is to produce the signal on one ear first and then the signal on the other ear. This fact is one of the best and most widely repeated in the literature: while Yntema and Trask were doing their experiments, others were being conducted by Gray and Wedderburn (1960) at Oxford, by myself and Margaret Gregory (1964) at Cambridge, by Bryden (1964) in Montreal, and most recently of all by a group of workers in Indiana (Emmerich *et al.* 1965). Everybody agrees on the answer, and there is no question that a mixture of classes of item changes the character of this experiment considerably.

Yntema and Trask argued that this difference suggested a different view of the original effect. Perhaps its explanation lay in the recall process and not in the original intake of information. They suggested that each item, as it was received, was given a 'tag' which could identify it if selective recall was desired. If all the items were essentially of the same type, the only different tags that could be given to different items would be those corresponding to the sense organ by which they arrived. Consequently, when recall was carried out, the organization of recall was likely to separate the items into those arriving at one ear and those arriving at the other. One might suppose that the recall operation takes the form of retrieving all items with a certain tag, and then going on to retrieve items with another tag. If, however, the items fall into two classes, if there are some letters and some digits, or some digits and some colour names, then there may be tags attached to the items on this basis also, as well as on that of the sense organ originally stimulated. Under these circumstances, the recall may be the colour names first and then the digits. Such at least is the type of theory which Yntema and Trask have put forward.

This kind of theory is undoubtedly much nearer the problems of a library or filing system than are most traditional theories of memory. It will explain other experimental results as well, such for instance as the phenomena of clustering which has been noticed by Bousfield in free recall of words (e.g. Bousfield and Cohen 1953). That is, if you give somebody a list of words and ask him to produce them in any order he pleases, he tends in fact to remember certain words together, because they are associated in his mind. This may happen regardless of the fact that you may not have presented them together, and that they are not required to be recalled in any particular order. This phenomenon would fit in very well with the idea that memory is divided into a number of separate storage areas, and that we can recall the items from any one of these areas fairly easily without disturbing other areas.

As we shall see in a moment, I do not think there is any doubt that selection does take place in retrieval, and that consequently its properties are of very considerable interest. Nevertheless, before I go on to that point, I ought perhaps to digress to say that I do not believe the original phenomenon which Yntema and Trask were considering to be one which disproves the existence of selection during perception as well as during retrieval. This is quite important, because the problem of the brain in perception is really very similar to that in retrieval: in both cases it is faced with far more information than it needs, and has to pick out some of it. The two selective processes may be closely similar, and although we are primarily interested in retrieval from memory on this occasion, I would not like to leave you with the impression that there is no selection at the time when information actually strikes the sense organs and goes further on into the brain.

The reasons for continuing to believe in the importance of selection during perception depend on facts which were not available to Yntema and Trask at the time when they put their theory forward. The key point is that the efficiency of recall in one order rather than another may depend upon experimental conditions at the time the material was presented: and these conditions must have had their effect during presentation rather than during recall. For example, suppose that some of the material presented is not going to be required in recall. Perhaps a man's voice and a woman's voice may be heard, and the experimenter asks only for the information spoken by the man. It makes a big difference to the efficiency of recall whether the person memorizing knows this at the time of presentation, or only just before recall is required. (Broadbent 1952; Broadbent and Gregory, unpublished). Therefore there must be a difference in the way the information is received and not just in the way it is recalled. Again, the speed at which material is presented affects these processes. To take one example, suppose I say to you 7 J 3 Q 9 R 5 A; this is harder to remember than J Q R A 7 3 9 5 provided that the speed of presentation is high. (Broadbent and Gregory 1964). It is hard to receive incoming items of different kinds in alternation at high speeds, but not at low. In terms of the library analogy, the librarian has to look at each book as it comes in, and if they arrive fast it is easier for him to put a whole group into one store before turning to a group of books for another store. There is selection in perception as well as in memory.

Let me now get back on to the main track of my argument, and recapitulate a bit about where we have got to. I started by drawing attention to the discrepancy between the organization of an actual library and the naïve view of memory as a continuous cinematograph film or tape recording of the series of events through which a man has lived. More sophisticated accounts of memory would alter our view about the detailed nature of the record, suggesting that it is composed of associations of input and output, and that it may economically consist of general rules together with particular crucial information-bearing items, but in many of us these sophistications leave the original analogy of the cine film untouched. In a library, however, the storage of materials may be physically in many different places, each of which is accumulating over time rather than in a single series. Furthermore, a second store is usually kept, arranged on a different basis from the ultimate store, and giving the place where one should look, the address, for each item under some reference tag such as the author's name. Yntema and Trask have suggested a similar organisation of human memory, because if you present people with material of two different kinds all mixed up, they can recall it separated out into the two kinds. At that point I digressed to argue that in fact the particular experiment which they were considering can now be interpreted rather as showing that the nervous system actually selects one type of material during presentation rather than during recall. It is, in terms of our library, as if the librarian on receiving a batch of books separates them by subject matter and then goes off to place on the shelves the books belonging to one topic before he comes back to deal with the remaining books. The grouping of items is produced to some extent during presentation rather than during retrieval.

Let me now take up the main theme again, and say that nevertheless Yntema and Trask's suggestion does seem to me to be correct for certain other situations. It is an addition to the selection of material in perception, but it is nevertheless a real effect. If we remain faithful to our previous arguments, we can show this by finding cases in which conditions at the time of presentation do not affect the efficiency of retrieval. One particularly interesting example of this is the case in which one presents six items, three to one ear and three to the other ear, but staggers the presentation so that each item on the left ear arrives at a time when there is in fact silence on the right ear, between two items. It was demonstrated some years ago by Moray (1960) that under these conditions people can very readily reproduce the six items in the actual order in which they arrived, rather than giving everything from one ear first. The explanation is presumably that in this case the listener does not adopt the rather artificial strategy of neglecting one ear and concentrating on the other, but rather behaves in a more normal fashion and listens to both ears simultaneously. In this situation, unlike that in which numbers arrive strictly simultaneously, he will not overload his perceptual mechanisms if he accepts the input from both ears at the same time. The interest of this situation from our point of view, however, is that selective recall can take place even although the listener was not aware at the time the material was delivered of the order in which it would be required. That is, we can either tell the listener to reproduce one ear first, or to reproduce in the actual order of arrival, and it makes no difference whether we tell him which we want before he hears the items or only at the time when we want him to recall them (Broadbent and Gregory 1961). This kind of selection must be operating in recall, and it certainly suggests that the items have been stored with a tag indicating the ear by which they were delivered. The process of retrieval can select the items that reached a certain ear, or the items that arrived first in point of time, with equal ease.

Here then we have a clear case of storage of information under particular tags or headings, by which it can later be retrieved. It is as if there were two shelves in our library, one marked 'Right ear' and one marked 'Left ear', so that each item can be stored in a separate place, and the contents of one store or shelf retrieved at one time. The more alert of you may have noticed a fault in the argument at this point, to which I shall return, but broadly speaking the picture of memory as organized in separate files under separate labels may be accepted for the moment.

At this point, perhaps I should digress to point to an analogy with the languages that are now used to program computers.

One can draw an analogy not only between the human nervous system and the library, but also between a computer and a library. Incoming information to a computer is placed in different regions of storage, just as different books are placed on different shelves, and subsequent operations may be carried out by extracting information from one area of storage, performing some operation upon it, and perhaps putting the result into some other area. In early machines the different areas of storage, the different shelves in the library, were known only by an arbitrary machine code, just as the shelves may be known as No. 3 North Wing or something of that sort. Nowadays, however, it is more usual to provide a system of communication with the computer whereby the programmer can attach labels of his own to certain areas of storage, and can then make statements using the labels in various combinations. Consider for example the illustration used earlier in the previous lecture of a statement such as 'Area:= length × breadth'. As we saw in that lecture this will be interpreted by the machine as an instruction to extract the information stored in that part of store which is labelled as 'Length', to do the same for the area of store labelled 'Breadth', multiply them together, and put the result in the part of store which is labelled 'Area'. In some cases, what is stored under a given label may include a reference to another label, and the contents of this second area of storage may include a reference to a third area, and so on. Very large amounts of information can be stored in this way, and the system of data may expand indefinitely which possesses considerable advantages for many purposes. The information contained under a particular label may take the form of instructions to perform some operation, as well as consisting of data such as numbers, so that by using a label such as 'SQRT' the programmer may call up a sequence of operations involved in finding a square root.

It seems to me a plausible analogy that human languages behave to some extent in similar ways, so that the making up of a simple affirmative statement to a man causes him to store in a labelled region of his memory information that has previously been available only under some other label. Thus when I say to you 'Mary is blonde' I am instructing you to transfer to the store labelled 'Mary' the information which at present you keep under the label 'blonde'. Parenthetically, this may include not simply neutral data, but also behavioural tendencies to react in certain ways to Mary. On this view, the importance of names and/or words in general is not so much the traditional point that they are stimuli which will replace the original real object or 'signs' of some real object in that sense, but rather that they indicate the location in memory of the information relevant to a certain topic or concept. Of course, not all labels for regions of memory need be of linguistic type: as I have just said, in computers the address of a particular area of storage may be either in a machine code, or in name assigned by a public language usable by many machines. In a library, the address of a particular part of storage may be 'No. 3 North Wing' (machine code) or 'The Linguistics Section' (public or user code). Equally in human beings one would suppose that there are some variables which are in a code private to a particular individual, and consist perhaps of particular sensory qualities difficult to put into any public language and communicate to one's fellow men. There are many people for whom certain numbers are associated with certain colours or shapes, for example, a smell may call up in one man memories of extreme significance while his neighbour is unaffected.

The point is an important one, because retrieval is not always perfect either in human beings or in the man-made systems which we have been considering. It is extremely plausible that in picking out a particular address in storage, one will occasionally go to the wrong address. But the errors which are made will presumably not be random, but rather will be linked to the way in which the different possible addresses are organized together. If one looks up a telephone number hastily in the book, it is the number above or below the wanted one which one is likely to get by mistake, rather than a number on the opposite page. If now labels for different parts of storage are to be used as means for picking out some memories rather than others, they too must be organized like the alphabetical order of names in a telephone book, so that a particular label will rapidly lead one to the correct memory. It is therefore not terribly surprising that, when a Conservative politician in Britain was being interviewed recently on TV by a Socialist journalist, called Paul Johnson, the politician persisted in referring to his interrogator as Howard Johnson. Nor is it surprising that most of us get the right message when we are told by Lewis Carroll that 'The slithy toves did gyre and gimble in the wabe'. When labels are closely similar, information under one will often be called up by the use of the other. Indeed, this kind of dependence of retrieval upon the structure which links together different labels for different types of storage can be illustrated from much of the classic psychological literature on human learning.

The view that I have been putting forward is not of course completely contradictory to, but rather a development of, the classic analysis of learning in terms of stimuli and responses. Although for reasons of time I have been talking mostly about experiments in a different tradition, this is not to deny the importance of the other stream of experimentation. Classic paired-associate experiments in human learning show that the extent to which two items of previously learned material interact varies with the similarity of the stimuli which elicit the items. Thus for example it is difficult for an English-speaking person to remember that the letter 'C' on a bathroom tap in France does not mean 'Cold': and we probably have more difficulty with this than would a German to whom 'C' on a tap means nothing previously. It is easy to remember that 'trottoir' is a word for 'sidewalk', but hard to remember that 'couloir' is not a word for 'refrigerator'. Similar effects appear of course even within one's own language: there are people who think that the adjective 'vicarious' means 'belonging to a minister of the Church of England'. These positive and negative transfer effects can be readily interpreted in terms of retrieval from memory of items stored in regions adjacent to the one desired.

By looking therefore at sources of difficulty in memory, we

may hope to find some signs of the way in which the storage is in fact classified and organized. One especially striking example of this has been giving rise to a good deal of work on both sides of the Atlantic during the past two or three years. One can present visually to a person certain information, and then compare the errors that he makes in remembering it with the errors that are made by other experimental subjects listening to the same information acoustically against a background of noise. The pattern of errors turns out to be closely similar in the two cases: that is to say, if a man is trying to remember a sequence of letters of the alphabet containing letters such as B C and D, he is likely to produce as mistaken items in his recall the letters V G and P. I may add that in the United States they also produce ZEE whereas we never do, because we call it ZED. All this is despite the fact that the letters have been presented visually and their shapes do not appear particularly similar; it is I think universally agreed that the person who is trying to remember them has converted the visual information to a memory that is structured acoustically, or, if you will, that he has said them to himself. A number of these studies have been carried out by Conrad in Cambridge, England (e.g. Conrad and Hull 1964), and it has been established by Wickelgren (1965) in Cambridge, Massachusetts, that the effects of transfer and interference, which I mentioned earlier, are in short-term memory especially serious if the new material is acoustically similar to the old. Thus we have here an example of the way in which the memory for visual events is laid out according to acoustic qualities, just as the names in a telephone book are laid out alphabetically.

I am leading up finally to an unpublished experiment, and would like to recapitulate my argument thus far. First, the problems of memory are not only those of storage, but also those of finding the right material again when you want it. Second, in man-made information retrieval systems it is essential to divide storage into many different categories, and also to construct an index. Third, experimental work on perception shows selection of particular classes of incoming information not only by sensory channel of arrival, but also by the category to which a word belongs. Fourth, a similar form of selection appears to operate not only during perception but also during recall. We can therefore to some extent think of memory as divided into separate stores from each of which we can retrieve separately by finding the right label. Fifth, the errors of retrieval shed some light on the classification into which memories are fitted, and in short-term memory the acoustic qualities, which an item would possess if it had been heard instead of seen, are relevant to such errors.

Let me now take up again the point which I said earlier had been loose in my argument. We can think of memories relevant to different topics as being stored in completely different places: say, on different shelves in a library. We may then think of retrieval as producing for recall the contents of one particular store, with a certain probability of extracting adjacent stores by mistake. But this carries with it the difficulty I mentioned earlier in connection with actual libraries, namely that one cannot operate on some other classification. If one store contains items A B C D, and another items R S T U, then it is difficult to retrieve a combination which consists of items B and S. But I mentioned an experiment in which words were presented in rapid alternation to two ears. I said that in that case it was possible to retrieve either in chronological order, or selectively by ears, as you pleased. This suggests rather that the items are stored, not in quite separate cells, but rather in a multi-dimensional lattice so that one can extract by different classifications.

In human terms, let us take the analogy of a set of personnel records which involves some male members of staff and some female ones. One might keep two separate sets of cards, one in one drawer of a cabinet and the other in another drawer. Inside each drawer, the cards might be arranged alphabetically or by length of service, but the two sexes would never meet. In an alternative arrangement, one might mix the cards within one drawer, but have a tag sticking up on the right hand side for male cards, and on the left hand side for female cards. The actual order of cards could be alphabetical or chronological as before. The advantage of this latter system is that it might well simplify extracting an alphabetical or chronological classification if one wanted such a grouping, while still making it possible to select by sex if one wished to do that. But the penalty which would be paid is that one might well, in selecting male cards beginning with the letter A, extract also the occasional female card because it happened to be adjacent to the male cards one wanted.

Let us now return to a psychological experiment by myself and Margaret Gregory. The technique was to flash on a screen eight items, all letters of the alphabet, but four in red and four in black. The subject was to be asked after presentation to recall either the four red items or the four black items but not both. Two conditions were compared, in each of which the same items were actually recalled. The difference between the two conditions lay in the irrelevant items, the ones that were not in fact recalled. In one condition these irrelevant items consisted of letters which had names acoustically very similar to the ones that were to be recalled. In the other condition, the irrelevant items had names which sounded quite different from the names of the items which were to be recalled. Now, if the memory of the red items and the memory of the black items had been stored completely separately, as it were in different drawers of a filing cabinet, there should have been no effect, upon the efficiency of recall, from the properties of those items which were in the other store. In fact, however, it is found that similarity between the red and black items in acoustic quality did increase the number of intrusions from the unwanted set of items into the ones that should have been recalled. In other words, short-term memory appears to be organized like the kind of personnel file in which the cards for men and women are kept in the same sequence, but with some mark on each card which allows one to pick out men only if one should wish.

Notice that we know this, not just because there are intrusions from the wrong set of items: that might simply mean that the labels from the two stores were hard to discriminate, or in concrete terms that the difference between red and black was hard to remember. But the number of intrusions increases when the items are close together on a quality which has nothing to do with the label by which the set of items is indicated. Going back to our analogy of the personnel file, if the male and female cards were kept in separate drawers and in order of length of service, we might get some female cards when we wanted male cards just by going to the wrong drawer. But we would not expect to find that this happened more often if men tended to have the same length of service as women, as compared with the condition when they had different length of service. An effect like that must mean that both male and female cards were ordered together by length of service. Similarly in our experiment, memory for red and black letters must be arranged in store according to the acoustic qualities as well as to the colour of the letters.

It is not at all surprising in fact to find that memory is not organized in a large number of quite separate stores divided up by successive classification like the Dewey Decimal System classification in a library. Even in libraries, such a system of classification is found unsatisfactory when pushed to the limit (Vickery 1965). For example, a particular book may seem to be appropriate to Psychology, and yet also to have relevance to Education, to Computer Science and to Library Retrieval. If it is put in only one of these subjects, it will not be retrieved by a system using only the single hierarchical classification. It is more general to say that each book has a number of characteristics, drawn from a large vocabulary of possible features which a book might have. The list of terms which say what characteristics a book may have are known as the descriptors of the book, and the hierarchical classification is a particular case in which the presence of one descriptor implies the presence of certain others and the absence of others. Thus in the hierarchical system if a book is described as Physics, it must also be Science, and is not allowed to be Biology.

In fact one can make a very large number of different hierarchies from any given set of descriptors by allowing some different combinations and disallowing others. For example, one might have a hierarchy in which one decided first of all if a book was psychological or not, and then divided those books which were psychological into those which were fact and those which were fiction, rather than doing it the other way round. Some people might think that this was a much more reasonable hierarchy. Indeed, instead of thinking of a library as divided into a vast number of small separate and completely independent sections by subjects, one might almost equally think of each book as potentially describable by a vast array of different adjectives, which indicate its characteristics. Sophisticated retrieval systems of the present day recognize this fact: they may well take account of restrictions between particular descriptors, such as the fact that in a given library there may be no books which are both Science and Fiction. But such restrictions are largely a function of the population of items that have to be classified for retrieval, and are not absolute properties like those in a traditional hierarchical classification. This allows one to cope with the modern situation in which a book on, say, the structure of the R.N.A. molecule may be regarded as Physics *and* Biology.

Our simple little experiment, therefore, on the effects of acoustic confusions between material that is primarily classified by its colour, goes to show that human memory is similar to these more sophisticated forms of information retrieval from libraries, and not to the simple hierarchical classification. In short-term memory, over a period of a few seconds or minutes, direct sensory qualities such as acoustic nature, colour, time of arrival, and so on are of great importance for the classification of memory. Relationships of meaning, which are not reflected directly in sensory quality are relatively less important: the words 'tranquil' and 'serene' are similar in meaning, while the word 'rugged' is similar to neither. Experiments by Baddeley and Dale (1966) in Cambridge show that similarities of this sort have relatively little effect on short-term memory, and thus cannot be supposed to form part of the system or structure in which the memories are located. In long-term memory, however, lasting over several days, this is not the case at all. Similarity of meaning then becomes exceedingly important in deciding whether there should be transfer or interference between old and new learning.

Thus the organization and labelling of memories which have been firmly established seems to be rather different from that of memories of recent acquisition and short duration. All the same, it seems likely that in long-term memory also it is possible to extract information by many different routes, rather than having it located purely in a single separate store. Let me take up in this connection a point I made earlier about the likely role of words as labels for particular forms of storage, and remind you of the remarkable properties of word-association. If you say to most people the word 'black', and ask them to say the first word which comes into their head, they will tend to say the word 'white'. At first sight you might think that this represents a frequent conjunction in experience, but if you think about it, it is rather odd that word associations of this sort very rarely represent, for example, prepositions or other functional words. In ordinary English sentences, one may talk frequently of 'The house in the valley' or 'The house by the sea', but if you say to a man 'House' he is most unlikely to reply 'In' or 'By'. It is quite a good bet that he will reply 'Garden', which is a word that could hardly ever have occurred as the next word in a sentence. Such associations are unlikely therefore to be explained simply by frequency of occurrence in succession in past experience. What they do resemble, as has been pointed out by Vickery, is the restriction of relationship which may exist in retrieval systems between commonly used descriptors. If information is wanted about houses, it may well be filed under the heading of Garden. More specifically, if a man inquires at a library for information under a certain heading, relevant material may be searched for not only under that heading, but also under terms which are opposite, super-ordinate or subordinate to the heading and so on: just as the common word associations to a stimulus word are often opposite, super-ordinate, or subordinate to the original stimulus. The network of associations between words which human beings possess looks not so much like the contents of a book when it is opened, as the cross referencing of a subject index which is being used to find a book. If this is indeed the case, it would confirm the picture of words as labels for stored information which I presented earlier.

I said in the beginning that I would not be able to give many answers to the problems of the organization of memory. My argument has pointed, however, to the process of learning as similar to that of a librarian coping with his library. As the information comes in, it has to be stored in an active fashion which requires some analysis and transformation of what has occurred. Thus visual information may be stored in acoustic fashion, and no doubt vice versa. The storage may be under different headings depending upon the subject matter which is being presented, and above all when retrieval takes place, it is not necessary for the person recalling to have available the one correct label under which a particular item has been stored. Rather one can reach the same item through different character-istics, and one may be reminded of an event in one's childhood sometimes by a smell, sometimes by the song of a bird, and some-times by a spoken phrase. But in the long term, it is the links between words which make available one type of memory when another has first been recalled.

In some sense, the whole of this talk represents a meditation on the awkward question which was asked me recently by a dis-tinguished classicist. The question was 'What are we doing when we educate somebody?' The answer is not at all obvious, because almost certainly we are not really establishing any great store of information. I do not now recall very much about the Punic Wars, and my daughter's homework reminds me only too well how much I have forgotten of the theorems of Euclid. In educa-tion, therefore, we are not loading books into the library. Could it be that we are writing the Index?

Aspects of Human Decision-Making

The theme of this Meeting of the Association is that of scientific policy, and from some points of view it might therefore have been natural if I had chosen to consider the field of national policy in the support of psychology itself. It is indeed quite interesting to consider what determines what relative proportion of the national effort goes towards one subject rather than another. This proportion does not result from a decision which is completely objective and determinate; because the distribution is different in different countries. Admittedly, one cannot fairly compare the number of psychologists in the United States with the number in Great Britain, because the wealth of the two countries is so different. Suppose, however, that within each country we look at the relative allocation of men between different subjects.

From the Willis Jackson Report (1966) we see, for example, that the number of mathematicians in Britain is of the same order as, but slightly less than, the number of physicists. The reports of the National Science Foundation (1960) of the United States show that the same is true there. On both sides of the Atlantic, apparently, the distribution of effort as between mathematics and physics is about the same. Some other comparisons of the same kind, however, give very different results on the two sides of the Atlantic. For example, a higher proportion of American scientists are employed in industry than in education, while in Britain the opposite is the case. Graduates in engineering are as common as those in science in the United States; whereas in Britain the universities (as opposed to the professional institutions) only turn out half as many first degrees in engineering as they do in science. These facts suggest a more favourable position in America for technology as a whole. Coming closer to home, one of the most striking differences between scientific manpower on the two sides of the Atlantic is that in the United States the number of psychologists is greater than the number of mathematicians, and almost equal to the number of physicists. If we take those with doctorates alone, there are actually more psychologists than physicists. In this country, on the other hand, the ratio is something like 6 or 7 to 1 in favour of physicists. I believe the discrepancy between the relative amounts of effort in the two countries is greater in psychology than in any other subject I have been able to discover.

It seems quite clear, therefore, that British policy is to put far more effort into physics than into psychology, while that in the United States is to put in about the same manpower into each field. You might well, therefore, have expected me to explore so interesting a divergence in policies in the two countries, and perhaps to spell out what it means in terms of unfilled posts in the National Health Service, in the care of our children, or even in the fields of equipment design and working conditions which are my own special concern.

However, I am going to leave you to draw these implications for yourselves. Instead, I am going to take this divergence in policy as an example of the way in which human decisions may come out in two entirely different ways when two different sets of people are involved. The allocation of scientific manpower is not forced upon a nation by some objective factor in the structure of knowledge or in that of the modern economy: it takes its origins in the minds of human beings. The way our rulers think, which I am afraid is very similar to the way in which the rest of us think, makes a great difference to our lives. I am therefore going to consider in this paper some of the approaches which are beginning to tell us a little more about the nature of these decisions.

To start historically, there may perhaps have been a brief period fifty years ago or so, when psychologists would have explained the decisions produced by a man in terms solely of his experience with various kinds of action in similar situations in the past. By analogy with the conditioning of dogs by Pavlov, one might have suggested that financial authorities have developed a response of giving resources in situations which have been success-ful in the past, and have extinguished the response of giving funds in cases which have had a less satisfactory outcome. Dogs learn to salivate to a bell if food usually follows the bell, and perhaps we should not think of ourselves as too remotely different in our nature from other vertebrates. Such a view would conjure up a marvellous vision of our masters feeling compelled to give funds to anyone who said that he wanted to invent the telephone or discover penicillin. To put that criticism more precisely, this kind of theory does not allow for the production of a correct response in a new situation, only in one that repeats itself. Fortunately therefore it is doubtful whether anybody ever really held such a view, and it has certainly been agreed for a very long time that something rather more complicated is needed to explain the behaviour of animals even as simple as the rat.

The story has been told on a number of occasions, but in brief the situation seems to be that an animal builds up inside its head a kind of map of the outside world which surrounds it (Broadbent 1961). When some problem arises, such as being thirsty and wanting to get to water in a particular place which has never been reached previously from this direction, the animal can compare different ways of achieving its goal by means of this map in its head. It will therefore be able to produce an appropriate and correct response even to a new problem. There has been a good deal of dispute about the exact conditions under which the map is built up, and particularly about the importance of reward in doing this. Some theorists regard the map as behaving rather like a stimulus from the outside world, while others regard it rather more like a response of the organism itself, and corres-pondingly rather different terms are used by people emphasizing

165

different points of view. Nevertheless, there is fairly widespread agreement that something of this sort goes on in the humble rat, and we need not therefore assume anything more simple in explaining human behaviour.

To put it more formally, inside a man information is stored concerning the relationships between events which have occurred to him in the past, so that if he now wishes to attain some particular event he may try out inside his brain a sequence of possible actions and see whether or not it does lead to the effect he wants. It would clearly be very simple to feed into a computer the information that turning left at a particular crossroads will lead one successfully to the High Street, Albert Place and Mafeking Row, whereas turning to the right will lead one to Sevastopol Gardens, Jubilee Terrace, and Coronation Street. If we are then presented with the problem of finding our way to the Rovers' Return, which is known to be in the neighbourhood of Coronation Street, we could ask the computer to find the way, and by trying out the consequences of each turn it could give us the correct answer without our actually needing to take a walk.

All this is straightforward enough, and has been known for some years. I now want, however, to introduce some of the advances of the last ten years or so. First of all, even this theory does not allow us to deal with new situations as well as human beings can do. The stored information we have inside our heads about the nature of the outside world cannot simply consist of sequences of events which we have met in the past. If it did, we would be unable to cope, for example, with the grammatical structure of language. You might imagine that a child learns grammar by hearing sequences of words which are allowed in English, and by being corrected for producing incorrect sequences. Suppose, however, I produce the following sentence 'The student, whom we admitted last year on the basis of rather poor examination results but with a very good Headmaster's report, and on the understanding that this was not to create a precedent of any sort whatsoever, *are* not doing very well so far.' It is likely that almost anybody who hears this sentence, and certainly anybody who reads it, will be able to tell that it is not a grammatical sentence: whereas if I had said 'The student etc., *is* not doing very well', the sentence would have been acceptable. However, the number of words in the sequence starting 'student' and finishing 'is' is so great that none of you are old enough to have heard all possible strings of words of this kind even if somebody had been reeling them off at you at the rate of one word a second ever since you were born. Clearly, therefore, our knowledge of the structure of language is not based upon experience of all possible strings of words; and, speaking technically, a finite state grammar is unsatisfactory. Even in cases where language is not involved, it becomes, therefore, rather doubtful whether we merely store the conditional probabilities of various combinations of events.

In the case of language, there has been a good deal of effort and indeed success, in producing other ways of formulating what we learn in grammar (Thomas 1965). These formulations are general rules for operating on sets of elements, and if they are followed we can produce any acceptable English sentence but no unacceptable ones. One class of such rules, for instance, consists of 'rewriting' rules. In these one lays down that, in any grammatical sentence, a particular type of element can be replaced by a string of other particular elements without making the sentence ungrammatical. Thus, in the sentence 'The student is not doing very well', one could replace 'student' by 'clever student' or by 'student whom we admitted, etc.', or by a variety of other possible substitutions. As these rules can be applied over and over again, sentences of indefinite length can be produced from a relatively small number of rules. There seems to me little question that this type of rule is psychologically real and important, not only in language but in other structured experience. For example, there are well-known experiments which show that an animal which has learned to run through a maze will swim through it on the first occasion when it encounters the maze half full of water, and it seems clear that the animal has learned the general rule that various means of locomotion can all be substituted for one another if the context is otherwise suitable. At a human level, one can see the effect of learning rules rather than specific associations when a child says that he wants to buy another mouse so as to have two 'mouses'; or that he has 'goed' across the road. It has to be general rules, rather than specific elements, which we learn: and in this we are of course similar to computers, which would much rather store away in their memories the procedure for calculating a square root than a complete table of all the square roots they might conceivably want.

In the study of language, the main uncertainty surrounds transformational rules, which state that a string of elements in one order can be replaced complete by a string in a different order. That is, if it is correct to say 'The cat sat on the mat' it is also correct to say 'The mat was sat on by the cat'. This type of rule is very attractive to linguists, as it leads to a very economical description of many peculiar features of the language. Various experimenters have produced evidence that this type of rule is also psychologically real. They have, for example, asked people to learn sentences like 'The ball was hit by the boy' and then shown that in memory this tends to be reproduced by a man as 'The boy hit the ball', which is grammatically a transformation of the same kernel string (Mehler 1963). Not all of us are happy, however, about the psychological reality of this kind of rule, because it is very difficult to see how it could easily be applied to the understanding of a sentence by ear, with each word arriving separately one after the other. In computer parlance, this would be a left-to-right analysis, at a single pass, and there is some difficulty in making use of transformational rules in a case of this sort without rather elaborate complications. The debate continues, but if I may be allowed a personal point of view, I would like to suggest that an active sentence may produce in the listener something of the nature of a visual image, which might well be reproduced from memory in the form of a passive sentence, or vice versa. More generally, the string of symbols which makes up a spoken sentence may be transformed into a multi-dimensional structure of information in the listener, from which a different one-dimen-

sional string of words might be retransformed. Now the transformational rules of linguists take the form of converting a one-
dimensional string of symbols directly to another one-dimensional
string. I would suggest, therefore, that such rules do not necessarily correspond directly to something in the brain, but that
there are psychological functions which partly overlap with the
linguistic rules.

Let me return now to the main line of argument. It is established that animals, and therefore presumably men, store up a
kind of map or model of the outside world inside their heads,
from which they can work out the consequences of various
possible actions in order to see which one gets them the thing they
want at the moment. We now know, from the theoretical
advances of grammarians and from experiments on human
language, that this model must often take the form of general
rules rather than of specific connections between particular
experiences, but that need not affect the general principle of
internal trial and error leading to the choice of the most satisfactory action. There is, however, another difficulty to be considered, and that is that one could not possibly in most real situations explore to the end all the possible lines of action. Even in
chess, for instance, there are many different moves which one can
make at any point, and to each of these there are many possible
answers which the opponent might make, many different further
steps one could proceed to employ oneself, and so on. To trace
out every one of the possibilities in order to see which led to
wins and which to losses would be quite inconceivable. Yet
chess, if the addicts will pardon me, is very considerably simpler
than many decisions in politics or business. We may sometimes
have our suspicions that actions in these latter fields are not
always taken successfully, but at least we know that human
beings can play chess, and joking apart, some of them seem to do
consistently well even in more complicated activities. How do
they do it?

At this stage, I want to distinguish two ways of solving problems. One of them is to go through some procedure which is

guaranteed to get the right answer in the end. For example, if I want to know somebody's telephone number, I go to the directory, look through the alphabetical sequence of names until I reach the one I want, and then look at the number on the right of that. The jargon word for this kind of procedure is *algorithm*.

The second way of solving problems is to take actions which are not guaranteed to give the right answer, but are more likely to do so than completely random action would be. For example, if I want to get a taxi in a strange town I may head for the railway station because taxis are usually there. Of course I might be wrong, and sometimes am, but it is on average a method of attack which works. Similarly, in deciding between different moves in chess there are certain principles which make it more likely that the ultimate result will be successful although they do not guarantee it. For example, a move which takes one's opponent's queen does not necessarily mean that one is going to win the game, but it makes it more likely. Similarly, a move which gives one control of the middle of the board makes it more likely that one will win in the end. By using these principles, one can simply follow out the consequences of the one or two moves, and decide which of the possible situations gives the best likelihood of winning. Certainty is not necessary, and if one only has a limited amount of time or computer space, one prefers to get on with only a good chance of winning. The jargon word for this kind of procedure is *heuristic*. The big question is, do human beings operate on similar principles?

David Marples (1960) has investigated the history of important decisions in industrial design, and has shown that often the design team sets down the different ways in which it might achieve its task, and then considers what problems are likely to emerge as each of these possibilities is pursued. Where the consequences have been worked out a little way, it usually becomes clear that some further problem of design will have to be solved. The decision as to which of the possibilities will really be pursued depends upon an estimate of the likelihood of success given the expected difficulties. When the decision is taken success is not guaranteed, but merely probable.

The decisions studied by Marples are those of business, and not of individuals. The most determined attempt to demonstrate that single human beings work on the lines I have been suggesting, comes from the work of Newell, Shaw and Simon (1958) (see also Newell and Simon 1959). They have devised a computer program which would solve problems in symbolic logic, by the use of strategies likely to be more successful than mere random activity. They also took the records of human beings who had been asked to solve the same problems, and to talk aloud while they did so. A man solving this kind of problem might produce remarks like, 'If I apply rule 7 I will get this thing over to the right-hand side of the problem. But then how can I get rid of this other letter? Oh, I see: rule 4.' The computer program was made to print out a step-by-step record of its activities, and when these were placed side by side with the records of the human subjects, the same kind of steps could be seen in the same order. To the extent that this was so, it seems that the computer program devised by Newell, Shaw and Simon had been using the same kind of sensible strategy as the man: in symbolic logic problems, if one is trying to prove an expression which has P on the right, and starting from an expression which has P on the left, then to apply a rule which moves P to the other side is likely to get one nearer to the solution.

Can we be sure then that people operate like the computer program? Some of us are not completely convinced by the evidence of Newell, Shaw and Simon, partly because the nature of the research makes it difficult to publish large quantities of statistical information which might make one confident that the agreement of program and man was not due to chance. Perhaps more serious is the feeling that, when a man tries out a series of rules on his logical problem, the hidden steps which cause him to drop one rule and pick up another might not be the same as those in a computer, even although the actual sequence of observable operations was the same. With this kind of qualification,

171

there can be little serious doubt that people do tackle problems by doing things which usually work and then looking to see whether they are nearer an answer.

We have now reached the important point that, when a man tries out inside his head each of the possible things he could do, he usually cannot hope to be certain of finding an action which will guarantee success. He looks only for something to do whose consequences will get him to a state which seems to him more probable to lead to ultimate success. The role of probability in decision is very frequently left out in everyday discussion. For example, it is no criticism of a political decision to say that one would rather be 'Red than Dead', unless the probability of Redness following action A is equal to that of Deadness following action B. An everyday example may make this even more clear. Early in 1967, Michael Lebrun, an eight-year-old boy living in the State of New York, was badly bitten by three dogs which escaped without anybody knowing which dogs they were (*Newsweek* 1967). Michael's father then had to decide whether or not to get the boy vaccinated against rabies. In this country rabies is effectively unknown, but in the State of New York this is unfortunately not so, and in 1966 seven dogs with the disease were found in that State. If Michael started to show symptoms of the disease, death would be almost certain. On the other hand, the course of injections is lengthy and painful. Just to make the decision more tricky, there is even a slight chance that something wrong with the vaccination might itself cause death through encephalitis. Michael's father in fact decided not to get his son vaccinated. Clearly he would rather have the boy uncomfortable for a few weeks than dead: but the point is that the discomfort was certain while the possibility of rabies, although perhaps larger than in England was still pretty remote. The family's medical advice in fact agreed with this decision, and agonizing as it must have been, it was rational. If we have to choose between a number of actions, and if we know for each action the probability with which it will lead to some event whose value to us we know, then on average we will do best by choosing that action for which the probability multiplied by the value is greatest.

To give another example of the principle, it would be marvellous if psychological research could discover a cure for pathological liars. This would be far more worth while than discovering the best method of arranging push buttons on push-button telephones. However, the probability in this day and age that a given investment of research will produce a cure for pathological lying is so low as to be hardly worth considering, while the probability that one can find the best arrangement of push buttons is very high. The more modest goal, therefore, is the sensible one at this instant; although I hope that none of us forgets that the other problem must be tackled as soon as our techniques are sharp enough.

The principle that one should go for the best combination of probability and value is a mathematical one: and again one could easily program a computer to do it. In this case, however, there is no doubt that people do not behave in the way which mathematics says would be ideal. If you give a man a choice between two actions and reward one action more than the other, he does frequently do the thing which wins more often, but he does not do it as much as he should do according to the mathematical ideal. (See, for example, Restle 1961.) I am not going to pursue this point very much, but it is worth noticing as the first discrepancy I have mentioned between the behaviour of a man on the one hand and of some ideal system on the other.

I want to expand upon a rather different kind of discrepancy, which may indeed be more serious. When we judge the probability of something, we may later get further evidence about it, and have to revise our judgments. For example, if we are military commanders and suspect that the enemy is about to launch a frontal attack on our position, we may receive reports from a spy that large numbers of troop-carrying aircraft are being moved up behind the enemy lines: and this obviously increases the probability that we are about to be taken in the rear by a parachute attack, rather than to receive a wave of tanks from the front. In real situations, one cannot work out quite what the probabilities are, and so one cannot assess whether the General is making his decisions correctly or not. In the laboratory, however, we can present a commander with a tactical exercise in which the probabilities are fixed and known, so that we can calculate just how much the judgments of the enemy's intentions should change with each new piece of information from spies or radio interception of enemy messages. Harold Dale from A.P.R.U. has done this and compared performance with the mathematic optimum (Dale 1966: Phillips and Edwards 1966). It is quite clear that a human judgment fails to shift the estimated probability of the enemy's intentions as fast as the incoming evidence should justify mathematically. The combination of probabilities from one's prior assumptions and from incoming evidence seems to be something which is especially difficult for human beings, and although they behave systematically and predictably, they are not doing exactly what would be expected from an ideally programmed computer.

We need, therefore, to know what it is about the working of the brain which makes it combine evidence badly. There is one process which might do this, and which I can best illustrate by an example. Suppose that you are sitting in the living-room, while your wife is washing up in the kitchen, perhaps to the accompaniment of a transistor radio. Suddenly you hear in rapid succession a crash of glass, an exclamation of surprise from your wife, a man's voice saying, 'Keep the dame quiet, Lofty' and a thump as if a body is striking the ground. Most of us would under these circumstances be inclined to draw the conclusion that something unusual was going on which required investigation: or perhaps needed a rapid departure through a window, depending upon the gallantry of our temperament. But now suppose that the same events had occurred separately and successively, separated by long intervals. You might well then have thought that the crash of glass was a normal accompaniment to washing up, that your wife's surprise was because the detergent had not run out after all, that the man's voice had come from a play on the transistor radio, and that the thump was really the contents of the laundry basket. Each of these conclusions would, for the particular evidence which it was designed to handle, be more probable than the alternative hypothesis that a burglar was in the kitchen. If, however, you had decided separately and successively about each of the pieces of evidence, and had then forgotten the evidence and remembered only your conclusion, you might well have continued to sit quite happily in the living-room, despite the fact that you have really had sufficient warning to take action. Actually, if you did take a quite independent decision about each of the four pieces of evidence, and if the odds were 10 to 1 against your doing something about each of them, the odds would have dropped to something in the region of 2 to 1 against by the time all four had happened. This, however, is not really getting the most out of the evidence: if the odds in Britain (even nowadays) are 1,000 to 1 against burglars in the kitchen, in the absence of any evidence of this kind, and if any one of the events reduces the odds to 10 to 1 against, then the presence of all four pieces of evidence makes the odds about 100,000 to 1 on for the presence of burglars. Obviously, therefore, one way in which a brain might fail to get value out of several pieces of evidence is to consider each one separately, perhaps serially one after the other, and to forget the original evidence after each decision but remember only the outcome. In some ways, a computer program operating on the lines of those proposed by Newell, Shaw and Simon might well do this, because such a program on existing computers normally considers each possible action successively rather than simultaneously. This is bound to mean that the load on memory capacity is large if all the original evidence for each step is stored, rather than only the final conclusions about a particular action: and the program might well take the latter course.

In fact, there is some evidence that people do handle certain problems by taking independent decisions and combining their results, rather than by adding together the evidence that is in front of them. A very simple case concerns the detection of inconspicuous signals. You will all remember the way in which submarine detection was done during the war by hearing the echo of sound signals bounding off the hull of the submarine. The same signal could equally well be presented visually. Now, we know that the perception of a faint sound is carried out by a mechanism analogous to a statistical decision: the ear presents to the brain some evidence, which points with a certain degree of certainty towards the presence or absence of a sound, and perception occurs if this evidence, in combination with prior information about the probability of a sound and its importance to the listener, exceeds some critical value. We know this from experiments which I need not perhaps digress to explain in detail, but which concerned the ways in which the number of correct perceptions of the sound vary when some experimental condition changes the number of incorrect perceptions (Broadbent and Gregory 1963: Swets 1964). But now, what happens if a man receives both kinds of signal simultaneously, if in fact he listens and also looks? If he makes an efficient use of the information from the eye and the ear, combining it together according to the best principles of mathematical statistics, his performance will improve to a very remarkable extent. This would be a case analogous to hearing the burglars in the kitchen with all four pieces of evidence simultaneously.

A petty officer might most readily hold an opposite theory of what would happen in simultaneous visual and auditory presentation, that failures in perception are due to the operator being asleep, and that consequently no improvement will occur if one gives him a different kind of display simultaneously. Between these two extremes there is the view that he will listen and look independently, and will report a signal if his decision either about what he sees or about what he hears should come out favourable. The improvement will be worth getting, but nothing like as great as it would be if he really made full use of the evidence he is receiving. This last theory is the one which experiments confirm (Brown and Hopkins 1967: Buckner and McGrath 1963: Loveless 1957). Colquhoun of A.P.R.U. has also shown in unpublished data that this applies within each of a number of people, rather than for the average of the group. If he can hear a faint sound on about half the occasions it occurs, and see a faint light on about the same proportion of trials, then if a signal consists of a light and a sound he will notice it on about 75 per cent of times it occurs. This supports the idea that separate rather than combined decisions take place.

Another line of evidence pointing the same way is through the perception of complex patterns. Suppose that a man is listening for a particular sound, such as the engine of a friend's car. The sound may have all sorts of separate qualities in it, such as a particular whine from the fan and a rattle from the exhaust. When the cars of other people drive past, which are similar in every way except that they do not have the same fan noise, then he quite often mistakes these cars for that of his friend. Similarly, he may do so with cars that are like his friend's in every way except in having the rattle of the exhaust. Suppose now that he hears a car which has neither the fan noise nor the rattle of the exhaust. Clearly he will be less likely to mistake this sound for the one he wants, but how much less likely? Can we suppose that he takes the two pieces of evidence quite separately and comes to a decision by each, or does he combine the two pieces of evidence in the best possible way? Derek Corcoran (1966) of A.P.R.U. has done such experiments, and there seems to be no doubt that, if we know the probability of deciding that two sounds are different in one respect, then we can predict the probability of deciding that two sounds are different which have two dimensions of difference, purely on the assumption that the two decisions are taken independently. Once again we are like the man who sits in the living-room hearing each of the events in the kitchen quite separately and successively.

The evidence I have mentioned so far shows only that the decision processes are sometimes independent, not necessarily that they are successive. However, by measuring reaction times one can sometimes hope to show that indeed processing of information has been serial in time. Let us take the analogy of an airport, in which the passengers arriving have to go through a Custom's examination to detect those who are carrying dutiable articles. It will of course always be a nuisance if there are more people on the aircraft, as it will increase the time taken to get away from the airport, but if everything dutiable is asked about simultaneously it will make no difference to one's avoidance of large aeroplanes whether the Customs are only interested in whisky, or also in perfume, cameras and tobacco. If, however, all these things have to be asked about serially and successively, the disadvantages of travelling on a large aircraft with lots of other passengers will become very much worse. Now let us think of a man's brain as the airport, the stimuli delivered to him as the passengers, and those stimuli which demand a reaction as passengers with dutiable articles. One can perform an experiment in which a man is given a number of letters to observe, and searches either for one, two, or more particular letters: Pat Rabbitt (1964) of A.P.R.U. has shown that when this is done with a high probability of a relevant letter being present, the time taken to search through a number of irrelevant letters increases as the number of relevant letters increases. That is, the brain works like a Customs man asking his questions successively, and not just saying 'Anything to declare?'

So far, I have tended to emphasize the evidence for serial and independent processing of decisions by the brain, with the consequent loss in efficiency of combination of evidence that may result. But on the other hand there is also very adequate evidence for simultaneous processing under other conditions. Rabbitt's experiment on searching for letters is closely similar to another one by Ulric Neisser (1963) who used a very low probability of having a relevant letter, and found that the time taken to search the irrelevant letters did *not* increase as the number of relevant ones went up. That is, sometimes the brain does behave like a Custom's man asking about everything simultaneously: Rabbitt (1966) has shown that the reason for the discrepancy is the probability of a relevant letter. If one is unlikely to have to do anything at all, one might as well find our first whether any action is called for, and only then what the particular action is. If on the other hand one is almost certain to have to do something, one might as well proceed straight away to finding out what it is one has to do. Parenthetically, I suspect that the Customs work on a similar principle, and shift from asking a series of questions to asking a broad simultaneous one, depending upon the probability that they are going to have to do something about it. Whether it is true or not of them, it is certainly true of the brain, and we do, therefore, sometimes operate simultaneously, and on logically separate decisions, in a way quite unlike the computer programs of Newell, Shaw and Simon because of the limitations of existing computers.

Lindsay and Lindsay (1966) also have produced an experiment which points in the same direction, by using a stimulus which might or might not have a large number of features. If they were all present there was one appropriate response; if all absent, another response: and if some were present and some were absent there was another response. If the subject had looked successively at each of the features, and decided separately about all of them, he could logically have made the last type of response faster than either of the other two. In fact, however, this was the slowest kind of response and this certainly makes it more likely that a judgment was proceeding simultaneously about all the features.

Another argument for simultaneous processing can be found in the perception of speech; some theorists have argued that we perceive each word in a sentence by attempting to match against the sound the most likely word in that context, and then correcting the first judgment if we are mistaken. This would be a serial process, and it would make certain predictions about the numbers of false perceptions in relation to the number of correct perceptions. I have myself provided some evidence earlier this year (Broadbent 1967) against such a view, and in favour of a simultaneous parallel comparison of the incoming sound with a whole range of possible words.

The implications of simultaneous processing in human beings have been emphasized in a provocative and stimulating way by Ulric Neisser himself (Neisser 1963). They remind us, as every generation needs reminding, that when we report by a single series of words what is going on in our minds we are doubtless telling only part of the story, because there are other and simultaneous activities going on which cannot readily be forced into a single stream in this way. This is likely to be more true at some times than at others, as is confirmed by the difference between Neisser's and Rabbitt's results when the experimental situation changes. We can all, however, confirm or deny from our own experience the extent to which we may be fragmented between a number of simultaneous and independent processes at some times, and highly integrated to a single purpose at others. It is increasingly likely that simultaneous processing will be built into computers as the years go by, because it possesses considerable advantages for certain purposes. It also of course possesses disadvantages, because it means that the results of one decision may not be available when another is taken: if two people are going out for the evening, and one decides how much money to take while the other simultaneously chooses where to go, they may end up at an interesting place without enough money. The existence of simultaneous processing, therefore, must act as a caution upon taking too literally models of the Newell, Shaw and Simon type. The choice of one course of action out of a number of others may not proceed from an analytic and successive calculation of advantage, but from a multi-dimensional structuring of information difficult to realize on existing generations of computers. Remember at this point my comments on the limitations of transformational grammar in the understanding of human language.

I am turning now towards the last section of this paper: you will recall that I started by pointing to the differences in decision which arise in different cultures, and by asserting that there is reasonable ground for believing that our brains calculate upon a model of the world the various consequences that will arise from different actions. The discrepancies which appear between our decisions and a mathematical ideal can be accounted for partly by our making separate independent decisions and combining the products rather than combining the original evidence, and by our carrying out certain processes simultaneously rather than successively. The results of the decisions are bound to reflect to a great extent the particular structure of information that is built into each one of us. In the space remaining, I must try to show how we can attack this structure and find out how it differs between one man and another, or indeed between one nation and another. I am going to give only one example, which does not go very far, but has the merit of consisting of experimental data gathered especially for this occasion. Not only that, but we have gathered data to present to you from sources separated pretty well as far as they can be on the surface of this earth.

It is of course almost a trivial task to ask somebody to indicate how far he thinks a certain adjective can be applied to a certain person or class of persons. For example, I could ask you to consider the adjective 'wise' and its opposite 'foolish', and to imagine a 7-point scale, of which 1 corresponded to the extreme of wisdom and 7 to the extreme of foolishness. The midpoint, where neither of these adjectives applied, would then be 4. I might then ask you to consider whereabouts on this scale a typical doctor was to be placed. This could then be repeated for other professions and for other sets of adjectives.

If one does this, for a dozen professions ranging from doctors to poets, and with a dozen or so sets of adjectives, one finds that certain adjectives seem to be used in rather similar ways. A profession which is regarded as wise tends also to be regarded as important, reputable, and so on. Professions which do not possess one of these qualities also tend not to possess the others. We may therefore say that to a great extent these different adjectives are being used in a similar way, and although they all have their own specific tone they are all also indicating the presence or absence of some common quality. By summing the scores for each profession on the adjectives in this group, we may therefore form a score which represents this common quality, and which can be labelled, roughly speaking, as the value which people set upon that profession.

There are of course other groups of words which behave in similar ways. For example, professions which are described as 'hard' also appear as 'strong' or 'masculine'. Again we can form a score which measures what is common to these various words, and forget for the moment about their specific qualities. The technique is one due to C. E. Osgood, and long familiar to psychologists under the name of the 'semantic differential' (Osgood, Suci and Tannenbaum 1957). From the point-of-view I have been urging, it sheds some light upon the way in which stored information is structured within the brain of the particular people who are being studied. Let us consider, for example, the way in which a number of professions appear when plotted in two dimensions, from the data from a number of Cambridge housewives.

A number of mildly amusing features emerge from this diagram: notice the high position of doctors on the value dimension, and the distinctly low impression held of poets, musicians, critics and politicians. This is the moment to indicate that we have obtained similar data not only from Cambridge housewives, from male and female Cambridge psychology students, but also

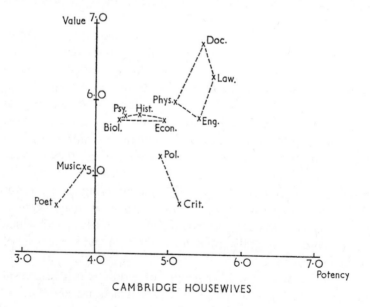

CAMBRIDGE HOUSEWIVES

FIG. 3

through Bob Travers from housewives in Kalamazoo in Michigan, through Frank Restle from psychology students – male and female – at the University of Indiana, and through Ian Reid from girl students, all of Japanese descent, at the University of Hawaii. In every case doctors were at the top of the value dimensions, and the four other professions that I mentioned were at the bottom, although they changed their order slightly between themselves.

The professions fall readily into four areas: doctors, lawyers, physicists and engineers clustered together in one area, while historians, economists, psychologists and biologists cluster in another rather less valuable and slightly softer. There remain politicians and critics, who are not particularly valued but are rather potent, while poets and musicians do not do well in value and are also regarded as distinctly soft. These four groups all held these relative positions in all the societies studied: as a quick comparison, consider the Kalamazoo housewives in Fig. 4.

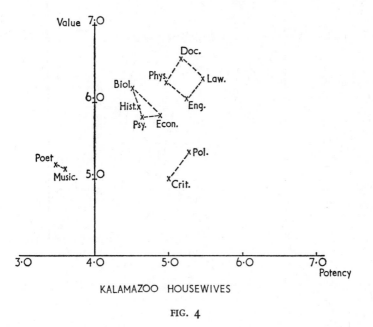

KALAMAZOO HOUSEWIVES

FIG. 4

If we take the rank order on the value dimension, the lowest correlation between any two of our widespread samples of people was greater than o·6, and in many cases the correlations were greater than o·8 or even o·9. There appears, therefore, to be quite remarkable unanimity of opinion in the attitudes of English-speaking people scattered over half the world: when one looks at the averages of fair-sized groups. In Fig. 5, we see the positions on the value dimension for each profession and each group: the professions are ordered by the order given by Cambridge housewives.

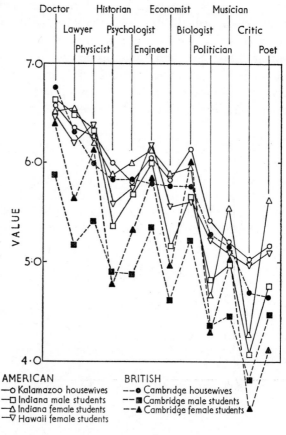

FIG. 5

Superimposed upon this remarkable degree of similarity, we do see certain slight differences depending upon the particular group that has been studied. For example, notice that housewives both in Cambridge and Kalamazoo regard politicians with a closely similar value, but that student groups both in the U.K. and the U.S.A. look on that profession with considerably less favour. Women tend on the whole to be relatively better disposed towards the softer subjects, and men to the harder ones. Last of all, there are just three professions in which there is no overlap between the American groups and British ones. In each case, the American groups have a more favourable attitude: and the three professions are – Physics, Engineering and Poetry.

You will remember that I started this paper by citing a number of instances in which the position of Science and Technology in the United States appeared more favourably and more widespread in society than it does in this country. It would seem that this favourable position is embedded in the way in which ordinary American citizens think of the different professions. When decisions are taken by men, the same problem is interpreted through different pictures of the world, and a different policy will result.

We do not know how it comes about that a man growing up in America develops a different structure to his stored information than does one growing up in Britain. It may be that, as some have suggested, the origins of these differences go back to fairly elementary reactions to particular personal qualities, built in during early childhood in family situations. This kind of thing may underlie the fact, for example, that humility and absence of aggression are seen in Cambridge as desirable qualities, whereas in Kalamazoo they are positively undesirable, and the correlations are opposite in direction. Whatever the origins of the differences, however, they demonstrably exist, and must be due to the society in which the people concerned live.

When, therefore, a man takes a decision on a question of scientific policy, it is likely that he works out inside his head the probable consequences of his actions. He cannot explore them all completely, but works on principles which are likely from past experience to produce success in the end. Once embarked on this world of probability, his choice may not obey completely the ideal rules for a mathematician. One reason for this is that he operates sometimes by a number of separate and independent decisions rather than truly combining all the evidence he gets. In addition, many of the processes involved are proceeding in parallel and, to use the popular but inexact and misleading term, are unconscious. Lastly, the very model of the world on which he is working reflects the assumptions of the society in which he lives. His decisions may well, therefore, be wrong, and it seems desirable to check them both by abstract calculation when one can, and by reference to the experience of other societies.

It seems to me that the level of support for psychology in this country and at this time is one topic which deserves very close examination in this way. To say that men are more important than cosmic rays, and that therefore they should be studied, is an example of an error which I have already criticized. If, however, I add the further statement that, at this moment, we have acquired techniques for the study of human beings which will show a large return for further investment in the subject, then I am no longer open to that criticism and it becomes very important to know why we put so many fewer people into psychology than do the Americans. (Our experiment sheds no light on this, incidentally. Perhaps we should have done it thirty years ago, when our present decision-makers were students!) Some of the techniques I have of course mentioned in passing: others are to be found in other papers presented to this section. I believe that these techniques should be extended widely and strongly: whether I am right is a purely intellectual decision, but I hope that it will not fall victim to the various hazards of human decision-making.

In Defence of Empirical Psychology

When men produce theories about human nature, the content of their theory frequently reflects the style of behaviour which they themselves favour. As a result, psychological theories are heavily influenced by the social climate in which they are stated. Competitive unplanned societies generate theories of random behaviour from which successful actions are selected by a survival of the fittest: highly organized societies, in which the community is everything and the individual nothing, tend to emphasize the integrated wholeness of behaviour. Even in individual psychologists, rather similar links can be seen between the way they work and the results they get: and it is because of this link that I am able to use a deliberate ambiguity in the title of this Lecture.

You may have wondered whether I meant by 'empirical psychology', a method or a theory. As a method, the term would mean that knowledge of human nature is to be gained by controlled experiment and observation, rather than by the intuitive exercise of the imagination. But the phrase 'empirical psychology' might equally mean a particular theory about human nature, rather than the method of arriving at that theory. The view in question is that our processes of thought reflect very largely the particular structure and dynamics of the world in which we happen to find ourselves. Such a view does not of course play down the extraordinary endowment which our nervous system provides; but it does say that the brain is remarkable in its ability to adjust to different experiences, rather than being remarkable by having an inherent structure through which it is able to handle the world. We are unusual in the efficiency of our learning, not in the pre-established organization of our thinking. You may have wondered therefore whether I wanted to support this empirical theory, or rather the empirical method.

In fact, I want to support both. Although quite a few people doubtless believe in one without upholding the other, there is some kind of correlation between the two. People who hold to the theory are perhaps a little more inclined to believe in the method than those who reject the theory. Belief both in the empirical method and in the empirical theory provides the twin basis of the behaviourist movement, and in defending both pillars, I am lining up on that side of the fence. I want to do so, because in recent years the opposite point of view has found a number of able spokesmen: and it seems to me that our society is swinging slightly against empiricism.

In our own laboratory, for example, my colleague Miss Pat Wright has conducted a survey and found that amongst those psychologists of roughly Senior Lecturer rank or above, about half called themselves behaviourists. But amongst those more junior, not one did so. I leave it to you to argue whether this was due to differences in scientific distinction, or just crusty old age.

If we look at the general intellectual scene, rather than specifically at psychological works, one can see signs of hostility to empiricism in several different fields. First, there is the popularity of a number of books drawing inferences from human behaviour from instinctive patterns in animals. In particular, there are the suggestions that human beings tend to defend territory as certain other species do, or that they have an innate tendency to show aggression. (See for example a review of a number of such books by Kathleen Nott (1969).)

Secondly, the more thoughtful magazines, broadcast programmes, and books seem nowadays to be full of warnings against the dangers of reductionism, the attempt to analyse human behaviour into separate distinguishable and comprehensible parts: and this warning is very often associated with the criticism that objective experiment on human beings may have morally undesirable results, because it involves treating them like machines. For example, the columnist R (1969) writing in *Encounter*, comments approvingly on an attack on experimental psychologists mounted by Chomsky; R says that 'The activities of behaviourist psychologists are something which everybody at the present time should regard with alarm and suspicion.' Again, in the foreword to the Penguin *Student Power*, (Cockburn 1968), there is a graphic description of the way in which ergonomists (which term includes applied experimental psychologists such as myself) tend to support the capitalist system. I shall come back to this question of the morality of the empirical method in human psychology, but for the moment I would just say that I think the advantage in human sensitivity and ethics lies with the empiricists and not with their opponents. It is interesting to remember, for example, that C. S. Myers, in whose name I am honoured to lecture, was exceedingly active between the wars in minimizing the harm done to workers by misguided methods of so-called rationalization and efficient management; and that his effectiveness in doing so came precisely from his ability to point to hard empirical evidence that early practitioners of time and motion study had misunderstood the nature of human beings. (My attention has been called to this point recently by Cyril Sofer.)

The third attack on empirical psychology which is obvious in the general culture is the one approved by R; that is, the linguistic approach exemplified by Chomsky. The general trend of that approach is to assert that 'Empiricist theories about language acquisition are refutable wherever they are clear' (Chomsky 1965), and that 'We must postulate an innate structure that is rich enough to account for the disparity between experience and knowledge' (Chomsky 1968). I think this point of view reflects a general drift in society, as the others do, but the linguistic wing of the whole movement seems to me much more interesting and relevant to human psychologists than the other divisions. For the rest of this lecture therefore I shall be talking about the psychology of language, and will say no more about innate aggressiveness or the merits of reductionism.

Let me give first a summary and inadequate account of what this school is saying. It arises from an attempt to produce an adequate grammar. That is, to produce a system of rules which will be infringed by those sentences agreed as ungrammatical: but which will nevertheless allow the generation of any of the infinite number of grammatical sentences. Such rules may be of two broad types: in the first of these, rewriting rules, a symbol may be replaced by a series of other symbols. Thus we may know that every sentence must contain a verb phrase *VP*, and the grammar may allow *VP* to be replaced either by v_i, an intransitive verb; or by $v_t + NP$, a transitive verb and a noun phrase. Again we may replace *NP* by a proper name, by an article and a noun, or various other possibilities. Thus we can generate sentences such as 'The boy runs', 'The boy hit Johnny', 'The boy hit the ball', and so on, which are grammatical. But the rules do not allow *VP* to be replaced by article $+ v_i +$ noun, so we cannot say 'The boy the runs ball'.

A different and more complicated type of rule is the transformational rule, in which a sequence of symbols is replaced by a different sequence in another order. We can illustrate the usefulness of such rules by considering the relation between active sentences, such as 'The boy hit the ball', and passive ones such as 'The ball was hit by the boy'. These sentences are related, but it is clearly difficult to generate the passive sentence from the active one, given only rewriting rules.

One might therefore try and use a transformational rule. Could one get the right result with a rule which acted upon the words themselves? Such a rule might change an active sentence into a corresponding passive sentence by moving the object of the sentence to the first position, inserting some form of the verb 'to be' in front of the verb of the active sentence, and then inserting 'by' after the verb and following it by the subject of the active sentence. While this might seem to work with the example we have given, it would not work if the active sentence was 'The boy was hitting the ball' or 'The boy is going to hit the ball'. In such cases the same rule working on the words themselves would give us extraordinary statements such as 'The ball was was hitting by the boy' or 'The ball is being gone to hit by the boy', or something of that sort. If we want to get the correct passive forms 'The ball was being hit by the boy' and 'The ball is going to be hit by the boy' by rules working on the sequence of words in the active sentence, we must have a different and quite specific transformational rule for each possible version of the active sentence.

A very much neater and tidier description of the situation can be produced by supposing that the transformational rule works with symbols more abstract than the series of words which appears in the spoken or written sentence. The specific words could be derived from a more abstract description of the sentence as a noun phrase followed by an optional auxiliary verb, by a transitive verb and by another noun phrase. The transformation rule changes the order of these abstract descriptions, and not merely that of the concrete and specific words. When this is done, the same transformational rule will allow each of the different possible forms of active sentence to produce its appropriate passive equivalent. We can see therefore that the use of a combination of rewriting rules and transformational rules will give a more parsimonious and appealing grammar, and that the language can be described much more conveniently in such a way.

Such a system of rules is, however, extremely highly organized, and it is especially important that the transformations do not act upon the surface structure of words actually appearing; but upon the deep structure of the underlying abstract symbols. Thinkers in this area have therefore tended to argue that the system is too complicated to be learned by the kind of learning machine which empiricists suppose, which assumes 'that only the procedures and mechanisms for the acquisition of knowledge constitute an innate property of the mind' (Chomsky 1965). The view derived from linguistics is rather that 'the general form of a system of knowledge is fixed in advance as a disposition of the mind' (Chomsky 1965).

If I am going to urge a rather different point of view, perhaps I should first make clear my attitude to this one. First, I regard the attempts to describe grammar in these terms as a great intellectual achievement, and am very conscious that most people working in this area are more intelligent than I am. Indeed, it seems to me that only a person of quite outstanding natural intelligence could possibly sustain the idea that the structure of the world is already present schematically in our minds in advance of experience, merely requiring to be realized and differentiated. Some of us have only too much experience from day to day of discovering that the world does not conform to the structure which we thought it to have. The descriptions of linguistic structure which have been produced following the example of Chomsky seem to me to be an enormous step forward, which I do not hesitate to compare with the advances introduced by Euclid into geometry.

But the analogy is chosen deliberately, because Euclidean geometry is an abstract system relating a large number of mathematical truths and deriving them from a few axioms. It does not, however, have any necessary empirical content: if two people set out from the equator on parallel courses towards the north, and rely on the empirical truth of Euclid, they will get a nasty shock when their paths cross at the North Pole. Similarly, I regard the transformationalist account of the structure of a language as quite abstract and separate from the actual organization of that language as a natural phenomenon.

Perhaps the distinction can be most clearly seen in the case of some non-linguistic behaviour. I have heard somewhere that Michelangelo,* when he called on someone and found them out, used to leave a visiting card containing nothing but a free-hand circle. The artist's ability to draw such a circle implies a quadratic equation relating the movement of his hand in one direction to movement in the direction at right angles to the first, $y^2 = K - x^2$. It also implies, perhaps with even greater simplicity, that the artist's hand travelled over a succession of points on the paper all

* My friends now tell me that it was Giotto.

of which were equidistant from the centre of the circle. From our knowledge of human skilled performance, however, it is exceedingly probable that the relationship embodied in Michelangelo's nervous system was neither of these, despite their simplicity and mathematical elegance. The control of movement seems to be in terms primarily of forces rather than positions, and correction of position error is intermittent and delayed. (See, for example, Noble *et al.* 1955; Briggs *et al.* 1957). A more plausible conjecture is that Michelangelo had learned a pattern of accelerations in two dimensions as a function of time, whose mathematical representation would be very complex. An over-simple possibility would be a pair of double differential equations, in each of which the acceleration in each dimension towards a reference point would be proportional to the distance away from that point. The phase relations need to be just right, which is why you have to be Michelangelo to do it. Mathematically such a description is apparently less tidy, but psychologically it seems more likely.

To take another example, multiplying 7 by 8 is mathematically equivalent to adding 7 to itself, and then repeating the operation six more times. On the other hand multiplication of two quantities can be represented as the determination of the quantity corresponding to the number 10 raised to a power equal to the sum of the powers to which 10 would have to be raised in order to equal each of the original quantities. The latter is in many ways a less elegant and parsimonious description than the former, but people usually do multiplication by using log tables rather than by repeated addition. Even more commonly they do it by reference to their rote memory of multiplication tables. That is, by an operation different from either description. Elegance of mathematical description of the effect of an operation does not bear any necessary relation to the empirical facts about the operation itself.

The distinction I am trying to make is a little similar to that which linguists sometimes make between competence and performance, that is, between the abstract knowledge of a grammar and its use on any particular occasion. Such a distinction must of course be made by any intelligent person, because most actual utterances are ungrammatical. I want to go further than the usual distinction between competence and performance, however, because that distinction still seems to suppose that linguistic competence represents a form of knowledge possessed by the language user. I see no reason why it should do so, except in the rather special sense that anybody who can add 2 and 2 may be said to 'know' Russell's theory of number. What such a person knows is rather a method of producing an outcome which can be described by Russell's theory: and it seems a pity to blur the distinction between the product and the process.

I regard the structure of transformationalist grammar, therefore, as an extremely useful and beautiful description of a body of utterances. But those utterances are produced by some mechanism which may well have a quite different basis of operation. As I have already shown, there is no necessary reason for supposing that a mathematically tidy description of the output will give one an insight into the deep underlying mechanism. The approach to language which I would advocate is a functional as opposed to a structural one. Let us regard each sentence as an instruction from one nervous system to another to carry out some action, including very probably the modification of stored information already present in the other brain. This view would not exclude the possibility of a man talking to himself, as part of his own internal operations, but I would hope that the principles would remain the same. The antithesis between this functional approach and the structural view of the linguists will probably become apparent as we go on.

Let me first strike at some points in the transformational account which seem to me weak, and to be so precisely because this approach plays down the importance of experiment and observation as a method. The attitude of the linguist is usually that any experienced user of the language, such as himself, knows the rules of grammar. Consequently he does not need to make observations of the actual use or understanding of sentences in order to establish his points. For example, a widely respected textbook of transformational grammar (Thomas 1965) gives the following sentence: 'When Bob and Pat come home, Bob puts Bob's car in Bob's and Pat's garage and Pat puts Pat's car in front of Bob's and Pat's house.'

This sentence is described as 'grossly ungrammatical'. The reason for this judgment may not be apparent to everybody at first sight, because my own verdict is that the sentence is perfectly grammatical, although it is certainly a little tedious and repetitious. A more elegant form would undoubtedly be 'When Bob and Pat come home, he puts his car in their garage and she puts her car in front of their house.' I can well imagine cases, however, in which it might be desirable to use the full names rather than the pronouns, and I personally would firmly describe the original sentence as grammatical. However, there is a reason for the textbook saying that it is not. It conflicts with a rule of some importance in transformational grammar, which requires the deletion or replacement by pronouns of repeated items. Without such a rule, many of the tidy descriptions produced by trans-formationalists will not work. For example, it is for many reasons a tidy description of the phrase 'A tall dark handsome stranger' to regard it as a combination by transformational rules of underlying sequences which might be represented as 'A stranger (the stranger is tall plus the stranger is dark plus the stranger is handsome)' . . . As part of the rules combining these various kernel sequences, one wants to delete parts which are repeated, or one will not get to the ultimate English form. Yet as a matter of empirical fact I am very unconvinced that deletion is obligatory in cases where it occurs in English sentences. It is there-fore rather odd to invoke it as an obligatory rule in a supposed transformational combination of kernel sentences.

I have not myself collected experimental evidence about the degree of grammaticality of Bob's and Pat's garage. However, I have done so in another instance involving deletion and the use of pronouns. This is a case given by Chomsky (1968): the key sentence is, 'Learning that John had won the race surprised him'. Chomsky asserts that the word 'him' in this sentence cannot refer to John. On the other hand, in the sentence 'Our learning that John had won the race surprised him', he holds that 'him can mean John. The distinction between these two sentences is important, because Chomsky's interpretation is entailed if deletion is carried out at a certain point in the sequence of transformations which build up the final sentence. Thus the assertion that one of these sentences cannot be understood in a certain way, but that the other can, is regarded as evidence for a cyclic application of rules in the generation of a sentence, and hence for the importance of transformational operations applied to deep structure.

Suppose we ask a number of people, such as Cambridge housewives or sailors, to look at a sentence like, 'Our learning that John had won the race surprised him'. We can then ask each person to indicate on a scale from 1 to 5 his judgment about the person meant by 'him'. A rating of 1 means that it is certainly John; a rating of 5 means that it is certainly someone else. Something in between indicates ambiguity, and obviously an average rating between 2 and 4 means that only a minority of people see the pronoun unambiguously. In fact with the sentence I have mentioned the average rating is 2·45. As Chomsky says, the pronoun may well refer to John, although equally it may not.

If, however, we try the sentence 'Learning that John had won the race surprised him', we find that the rating rises, highly significantly on statistical analysis. The pronoun is now distinctly less likely to refer to John. But the rating is still only 3·60, less than one unit from the point of complete uncertainty; this sentence does not exclude the possibility that John was the person surprised. Only a minority of subjects are sure that John could not have been that person. It is going too far therefore to follow Chomsky and say that the pronoun has been inserted at a certain stage in an abstract underlying process; if his arguments were correct, it should have been impossible for John to be the person meant by the pronoun.

This empirical result does not stem from a general fogginess or unwillingness of the subject to make a definite judgment. One can get a rating as high as 4·29 (almost certainly not John) for sentences such as 'John beat Tom because of his recent injury'. A rating as low as 1·14 (almost certainly John) is given on the other hand to 'John beat Tom because of his thorough training'. In these cases it is semantics rather than syntax which resolves the ambiguity.

One can get a corresponding lack of ambiguity simply from the order in which the names and pronouns occur. If we heard 'John was surprised that he had won the race', we regard John as the winner (rating 1·54). If the two clauses are in the opposite order so that John has not been named when the pronoun occurs, the rating rises significantly. Incidentally, Fowler warns against putting pronouns before their principals, in his *Modern English Usage*, although Chomsky rightly holds that the pronoun *may* refer to a following name.

My own view would be that the use of names in a sentence indicates the regions or sections of the recipient's memory which are to be involved in the operations he is to perform; and that a pronoun tends to be referred to the earliest possible region. Thus one can produce two sentences with the same meaning 'John told Tom that he had won the race' and 'Tom was told by John that he had won the race'; but the ratings in the two cases differ significantly, being 2·86 and 3·66. The first of two names is the more likely to be regarded as the person meant by the pronoun. It is this effect of order which gives the slight difference between the two sentences which Chomsky held to be unambiguously different.

In the light of these experimental findings, perhaps we should look again at the role of deletions and transformations in analysing a sentence such as 'The stranger was tall, dark, and handsome'. One of the reasons why transformational rules are so neat in analysing this sentence is that it is difficult to produce a description of it in terms of rewriting rules which are 'context free'. That is, we cannot produce the sentence by a rule which says that any adjective can be replaced by two adjectives connected by the word 'and', because that would only generate the sentence 'The stranger was tall and dark and handsome'. For similar reasons, we cannot get where we wish by using a rule which replaced any adjective by two adjectives with a comma between them. Nor can we simply have both rules and say that one can use whichever one wishes: that after all would allow 'The stranger was tall and dark, handsome', which we all agree to be ungrammatical (I hope). A transformational account can, however, readily allow for the introduction of a conjunction at any one point in the sentence: hence its superiority over rewriting rules.

In this analysis, however, we have assumed that the rewriting rules cannot take account of the other elements in the sentence, adjacent to the one which is being replaced. One could quite well have context-sensitive rules, in which an adjective could be replaced by two adjectives joined by 'and' *unless* there is another adjective following the one to be replaced. If one is allowed to use rules of this kind, where items that have gone earlier or which are just about to appear alter the substitutions which can be made, then it was agreed by Chomsky and Miller (1963) that one can probably do without transformational rules, by introducing different *ad hoc* rules for each of a number of problems such as that of combining adjectives. The reason for preferring transformations is rather that they give a simpler and more elegant pattern. Remember the relation between actives and passives which we have already considered.

Yet if one turns attention away from the abstract structure of the language, and rather considers a brain, a computer, or some other system receiving and generating strings of words in real time, then it is very reasonable that the rules being applied at any instant should depend upon the items just produced or just about to be produced. Indeed, we saw in the experiment on pronouns some reason to suppose the brain understands the pronoun with reference to the sequence of the people or objects named in the sentence, and not so much with reference to the successive transformations which might produce this sentence from the underlying deep structure. It may be a good idea therefore to turn again to the question of active and passive sentences, and, instead of looking at the simplest possible relation between them, let us consider rather the effects which each type of sentence produces upon the listener who receives it.

Experiments of this kind have been carried out by Tannenbaum and Williams (1968) and by Wright (1969). In each case, the person being tested received sentences which might be active or passive. In Wright's experiment they were then asked a question about the content of the sentence. That is, they received 'The boy hit the ball' and were asked 'Who hit the ball?'. Tannenbaum and Williams did not use natural question forms: rather, in testing memory they gave sentences of active or passive type, but with gaps for two of the three possible content words in the original sentences (that is, they supplied either the subject, or the verb, or the object). With either of these techniques, one can make some comparisons of great interest. If active and passive sentences are both understood by being transformed to their underlying deep structure, then one of two things should happen. It might be that it would make little difference whether actives or passives were involved: since the memory is always for the unchanging deep structure. Alternatively, it might be that the decoding of a passive sentence or question involved some steps and transformations more difficult than those for an active form. What one would not expect on transformationalist theory is the result which actually appears: passive questions are easier with passive sentences than active questions are, and vice versa. If you have been told that 'The ball was hit by the boy', it is easier to be asked 'What was hit by the boy?' than 'What did the boy hit?'

What these experiments show is that there is a definite difference between the active and passive versions of a sentence, in terms of the effect which is produced upon the listener. To a pure logician, it may be that both sentences 'mean' the same thing: or to a transformationalist it may be true that both are versions of the same deep structure. Nevertheless, the changes produced in the listener are different. Tannenbaum and Williams represent this difference in terms of a 'conceptual focus', which is supposed to be set up by the earlier words in the sentence, and thus is different for active and for passive sentences. In support of this, they point out that the results show better memory when the earlier words in the sentence are used in the subsequent question.

That is, if you have received the sentence 'The boy hit the ball' you are better equipped for later questions which ask you what you know about the boy; while if you have received the sentence 'The ball was hit by the boy' you are better equipped for later questions about the ball. In terms of my own attitudes, I would say that the earlier words in the sentence indicate the region of memory which is to be operated upon as a result of receiving the complete sentence, and that the active and passive versions are not therefore equivalent in their effects upon the listener.

Parenthetically, one ought to note that there are features of these experiments which certainly show that the sentences are remembered in terms of their meaning, rather than merely as a string of words. For example, in Wright's technique, by contrast to that of Tannenbaum and Williams, only one word is needed to answer the question. Even if sentence and question were given in passive form, memory is better if the word required is the one which would be the subject of the active form of the sentence. It seems sensible to interpret this result as showing a closer relationship of meaning between an action and the person who performs it rather than the person who merely suffers it. This in itself might be taken as evidence for a transformationalist theory, but it seems at least as plausible that it is a semantic rather than a syntactic relationship. (A similar result applies in our pronoun experiment: if John tells Tom that 'he' won a race there is a tendency for 'he' to be the teller rather than the told, as well as a tendency for 'he' to be the first person named.)

Let us summarize the position thus far. First, we have seen that the modern rationalist thinks the empirical theory unsatisfactory because of the complexity of the transformational rules that he prefers to describe language, and the fact that these rules apply to deep structures not apparent in the actual string of words experienced. Secondly, we have challenged this particular view by denying that the best abstract account of language is necessarily a good account of the processes producing the language. Thirdly, we have seen that certain key points in the transformational approach seem a little weak in their empirical support. In particular, this applies to deletions and the use of pronouns; pronouns are interpreted rather in terms of the sequence in which words have occurred than in terms of the underlying structures of the trans-formationalists. Fourthly, we have seen that context-sensitive rules can quite well be used to give accounts of those phenomena explained transformationally, but that the resulting system is less tidy as an abstract structure. Fifthly, experimental evidence casts some doubt upon the psychological reality of derivation of active and passive sentences from the same underlying kernel. Rather, the effect upon the listener depends again upon the sequence in which particular words are perceived.

If now I want to round this argument off on lines which sup-port empiricism, the main difficulty to which I ought to address myself is the *learning* of the relationship between active and passive sentences. You will remember that a single transformation will produce the corresponding passive from any active, and that accordingly it seems reasonable to suppose that an adult English speaker has learned the transformation relationship: it is part of his competence. It is certainly very unlikely that he has learned by experiencing each of the specific sequences of words which are allowed, and that he has been corrected for producing incorrect sequences. The number of sequences of words which would need to be involved would be impossibly large.

In turning to this topic, one must point out an interesting failure of communication which seems to have existed between linguists on the one hand and those psychologists interested in animal learning on the other. It seems to have been supposed by linguists that an association between two events (a) and (b) must always involve all the features of (a) and all those of (b). Thus they treat it as absurd that one should learn by the ordinary principles of animal learning to refrain from producing sentences such as 'The old grey mare are not what he used to be', because one is unlikely to have met many sentences which start with the same four words as the example. Experimenters in the field of animal learning have long supposed, however, that the animal learns only the relations between selected parts of the surroundings: some theorists refer to this selection as the use of observing responses, some as the switching in of analysers, but almost all of them make some provision for a selective operation upon the vast quantity of information striking the sense organs. Thus what rats learn in a discrimination experiment is by no means that food is associated with a large red square on the right-hand side of the field of view, on 22 March with the sun well above the yard-arm. On the contrary, they learn that the whole class of square shapes, regardless of position or of other qualities, is to be associated with food. Furthermore, the response appropriate to obtaining the food is not a single isolated muscle twitch, but rather an enormously elaborate and creative sequence which may be quite different on each occasion it appears. What is learned by animals is not therefore an association between one concrete event and another concrete event, but rather between two conceptual classes, each of which may contain any one of a large number of members. All this has long been established and agreed by workers calling themselves behaviourists, long before linguists became interested in psychological topics.

If therefore human beings learn by the same process as animals, we would not expect them merely to associate a particular word with the particular word that happens to follow it on one specific occasion. Rather we would expect them to treat a word or a short sequence of words as a member of a class, and to know that any member of a particular class requires the same operation within the brain. We would also expect them to learn the sequences of classes. Some sequences of individual items would then be recognized as legitimate, even though they had never occurred previously in conjunction with each other, because they were recognized as possessing those features which form a legitimate sequence.

I have already pointed out the reason for the parsimony of the transformational account of the relation between active and passive sentences. It arises because each of the different forms of an active sentence can be derived from the same abstract sequence of symbols, and similarly that there is another single abstract sequence for the forms of a passive sentence. Only for that reason does a single transformation relate the active to the passive at the abstract level. Thus from an empirical point of view the correct analysis is not to suppose that the human being learns a mysterious transformation rule, which does not operate on the concrete series of words experienced: but rather that the pupil learns each of the forms of an active sentence as instances of the same sequence of abstract descriptions. To learn the same abstract sequence as applying to all the forms of active sentence, and to learn another abstract sequence as applying to all those of passive sentence, is automatically to acquire behaviour describable by a single transformation rule.

The factual question which needs to be examined then is whether indeed learning can take the place of the relationship between two groups of words, when the particular words tested have never concretely been associated with each other in experience. Some experiments showing this for artificial languages have been performed by Braine (1963), whose views bear a family relationship to my own. (The differences are on points such as my more explicit emphasis on selectivity in learning. Braine also writes slightly as if the response to a class of words was another word, whereas I am emphasizing that a class of words is learned as requiring a particular class of operations within the brain.) It is, perhaps, closer to real life to take another experiment, by Torrey (1969), which used a real language. In this experiment Russian sentences were learned, either by explicit instruction in the principles of the grammar, or by a more direct process des-cribed (perhaps unfortunately) as 'drill'. In this latter process the pupil experienced a set of Russian sentences each of which could be divided into parts. Grammatically, the words from the first part of one sentence could be combined with the second part of the other sentence, as if in English one were to use sentences such as 'The boy/ran quickly, the girl/ate hungrily, our friend/came yesterday'. In testing the degree of attainment of those instructed in grammatical rules, and of those who had been drilled, test sentences were used which contained elements never previously associated with each other. Yet the best performance on these sentences was produced by the pupils who had learnt by the so-called drill method. That is, they experienced Russian words in appropriate serial positions in a series of sentences, and afterwards they could use new sentences combining words correctly. There is no question therefore that words can be learned as members of a class which belongs in a certain serial position, and that learning of this type can produce the ability to construct entirely new sentences. It is worth recalling that the first step in a child's language is often a simplified or 'pivotal' grammar, in which each utterance consists of two parts (Brown and Fraser 1963). The first part is one of a list of possible words, and the second is chosen from another list. Thus we get utterances such as 'Daddy gone, Johnny cold, Daddy cold, Johnny gone' and so on. This simple grammar is not of course adequate to explain the complexity of adult language, and it could be argued that a learning of the order of abstract classes, on the lines described earlier, could not explain the ability to understand and construct sentences such as 'The boy, who did this, that, and the other, hit the ball', because the string of words following 'who' can be very long indeed.

Once again, however, this point is only a difficulty if one assumes that every event striking the ear is learned unselectively. The evidence is rather that an actual brain records only the occurrence of certain features of certain events in its surroundings, and stores the degree of relationship between those features only, ignoring any other stimuli which may happen to strike it. In the establishment therefore of the correct relationship between 'Boy' and 'hit', so that we recognize that it would be wrong to say 'are hitting', it is by no means necessary that the occurrence of a number of other intervening events should be a hindrance. The comparison with animal learning would suggest that a relationship would only be learned between those items for which there was an observing response or analyser in operation. Thus even non-human animals are endowed with methods of learning which remove this particular difficulty for empiricism.

A further interesting question is raised by our own superiority over animals: perhaps that superiority might be in the ability to form classes of classes recursively to a higher degree than animals, or perhaps as Morton (1969b) suggests in the ability to hold in store a relationship conflicting with present experience. These valuable endowments of procedure and mechanisms of learning may give us an advantage over animals. But a proper respect for the complexity even of animal learning suggests that there is no need to suppose an innate endowment of linguistic structure.

In general, therefore, I cannot support the idea that the amount of information which a child receives in sentences spoken by its mother and other adults, is too small to allow grammar to be learned by an empirical process. On the contrary, there is direct evidence from learning experiments that the ability to construct sentences can be acquired from methods of training organized on the assumption that the sequence of classes of utterance is acquired empirically. I have also given you reasons for thinking that a transformational account of language is not sufficient in the other sense of empirically. Of course I hope I have made it quite clear that I find such a grammar a useful description of the structure of utterances, provided that it is not taken as an indication of the way those utterances are produced or understood. In visual experiments, we should be hard put to study perception without having geometric descriptions of circles and parallel lines: even though these descriptions bear little relation to events within the nervous system. Furthermore, I cannot possibly claim to have defeated Chomsky's dictum that specific empiricist theories are refutable, because I find I cannot be specific at a number of crucial points.

One must, however, compare the empiricist view with its opponents, rather than find fault with it in isolation. If we say merely that the structure of certain behaviour is, in some general way, built into the brain I find this also lacking as a specific explanation. I think therefore that I would regard empiricist views of the kind I have been putting forward as more satisfactory than any alternatives, until some indication is given at least of the elements of that universal grammar which is supposed to be innate, and preferably of the ways and the stages in which these elements are incorporated into the processing of information in the nervous system. I am not asking for a wiring diagram of the brain, but merely for a flow chart with the innate portions indicated. In the absence of such suggestions, the empiricist case seems to me better made than the idealist one.

Let me return to my beginning, and say that I do not think these questions can be answered without experiment and observation on actual human performance. I promised earlier to take up again the question of the moral quality of such experiments, and I said that I thought it would be preferable to use an empiricist method than any of its alternatives. We can tell nothing of our fellow men except by seeing what they do or say in particular circumstances. If one dispenses with this procedure, and so claims to be treating other people as persons rather than machines, one is exposed to the danger of assuming that everybody should be the kind of person one is oneself. In the best of human reasoning and imagination, there is a region of uncertainty because of difficulties of definition, of emotional bias, or of habits of thought: and in the physical sciences the explosive rise of the experimental method in the seventeenth century was a reaction against the savage inhumanity which had burst upon the world as a result of dogmatic theorizing.

So equally, in dealing with human beings, a proper sensitivity to other men demands that we should take an interest in what they actually do rather than what we think they do. The empirical method is a way of reconciling differences. If one rejects it, the only way of dealing with a disagreement is by emotional polemic. If somebody disagrees with us, the reason may well lie in the uncertainties of definition and the experience which I have mentioned: but in the absence of empiricism, our reaction is only too likely to be that he is intellectually defective or morally oblique. I do not think it accidental that much discussion on psychological topics by linguists carries a tone of hostility and polemic far more noticeable than anything which has been seen in psychology since the warring schools of the era when the subject was emerging from philosophy. In the works of intellectually distinguished linguists we may see the concepts of their opponents described as 'a mere phrase without any describable content' or a 'strange belief', while a preference for a different set of definitions becomes 'inability to conceive of another sense' or that the scholar concerned 'refuses to consider the question'. Emotionally charged words such as 'trivial' or 'incoherent' are frequent. It seems to me inevitable that an approach to psychology through the armchair, by the exercise of fallible human reason, intuition and imagination, will lead one to such hostility and disagreement with other people. If we refuse to use experiment and observation on other human beings, we start to regard them as wicked or foolish. I think this is a serious danger, and I have no doubt whatever that the methods of empirical psychology are socially more hygienic, or to use the older and more robust phrase, morally better. For that reason, I do rather regret that so much of this lecture has been taken up by conceptual analysis rather than by experimental results: but I hope at least that you may profit by the horrible example, and go out convinced to prove me wrong by the methods of empirical psychology.

Postscript

Since the preceding Lecture was given, some of my friends and colleagues have expressed surprise at some of the points made. In particular, they had not realized that Chomsky had intended his linguistic formulations to have psychological reality; nor that he had expressed views critical of empirical method. They therefore felt that some of the foregoing phrases misrepresented his position.

It should be emphasized therefore that Chomsky has in various places made the claim that his grammatical structures are features of the ground plan of a hypothetical mechanism: particularly, Chomsky (1965) page 9 and page 53. He claims also that this structure is present schematically in the mind before learning, for example in Chomsky (1965) page 76, paragraph 2, page 64 last paragraph. It should be emphasized yet again that I have no quarrel with Chomsky's linguistics as such, only with the belief that they have a psychological reality.

So far as Chomsky's attitude to empirical method is concerned, reference should be made to Chomsky (1965) page 19, lines 11 to 18 and 28 to 31: page 20, lines 1 to 3 and 12 to 15. See also Chomsky (1968) page 64, lines 5 to 14 and page 86, lines 2 to 6. The key suggestion of these passages is that the concept of grammaticality, along with other basic ideas such as competence and performance, must be defined intuitively: rather than operationally. It is then not possible to establish an objective standard of grammaticality by, for example, taking judgments given on particular sentences by a large panel of speakers of the language.

Chomsky adopts this position on proper grounds of logical

consistency, because he is concerned with the rules governing natural rather than artificial language, and it is certainly the case that people can learn as an intellectual exercise rules which do not occur in natural language (Chomsky 1965, p. 56). Thus judgments about sentences are not satisfactory as a criterion for his purposes. On the other hand, Chomsky does not wish to include as grammatical all sentences uttered or understood by human beings, because some such sentences may be imperfect for reasons such as memory failures or distraction (Chomsky 1965, p. 3). He therefore adheres to the procedure of defining the corpus of grammatical sentences intuitively: an entirely reasonable procedure for linguistic purposes. Psychologists who are naturally impressed by Chomsky's contributions to linguistics do not always seem however to have realised this particular aspect of his thought; which creates for psychological applications a number of difficulties, of which the ones given in the foregoing lecture are an example.

References

ANISFELD, M. (1968) 'Subjective approximation of relative letter incidence in pleasant and unpleasant English words', *J. verb. Learn. verb. Behav.*, **7**, 33–40.

AUDLEY, R. J. (1970) 'Choosing', *Bull Brit. Psychol. Soc.*, **80**, 177–91.

AUDLEY, R. J., and PIKE, A. R. (1965) 'Some alternative stochastic models of choice', *Brit. J. math. stat. Psychol.*, **18**, 207–25.

BADDELEY, A. D., and DALE, H. C. A. (1966) 'The effect of semantic similarity in long and short-term memory', *J. verb. Learn. verb. Behav.*, **5**, 417–20.

BOUSFIELD, W. A., and COHEN, B. H. (1953) 'The effects of reinforcement on the occurrence of clustering in the recall of randomly arranged associates', *J. Psychol.*, **36**, 67–81.

BRAINE, M. D. S. (1963) 'On learning the grammatical order of words', *Psychol. Rev.*, **70**, 323–48.

BRIGGS, G. E., FITTS, P. M., and BAHRICK, H. P. (1957) 'Effects of force and amplitude cues on learning and performance, in a complex tracking task', *J. exp. Psychol.*, **54**, 262–8.

BRILL, A. A. (1944) *Freud's Contribution to Psychiatry.* New York: Norton.

BROADBENT, D. E. (1952) 'Listening to one of two synchronous messages', *J. exp. Psychol.*, **44**, 51–5.

BROADBENT, D. E. (1954) 'The role of auditory localisation in attention and memory span', *J. exp. Psychol.*, **47**, 191–6.

BROADBENT, D. E. (1958) *Perception and Communication.* London: Pergamon.

BROADBENT, D. E. (1961) *Behaviour.* London: Eyre & Spottiswoode.

BROADBENT, D. E. (1967) 'Word-frequency effect and response bias', *Psychol. Rev.*, **74**, 1–15

BROADBENT, D. E. (1970a) 'Psychological aspects of short-term and long-term memory', *Proc. Roy. Soc. B.* **175**, 333–50.

BROADBENT, D. E. (1970b) in Mostosky, D. (ed.) *Attention: contemporary theories and analysis.* New York: Appleton Century Crofts.

BROADBENT, D. E. (1971) *Decision and Stress.* London: Academic Press.

BROADBENT, D. E., and GREGORY, M. (1961) 'On the recall of stimuli presented alternately to two sense organs', *Quart. J. exp. Psychol.*, **13**, 103–9.

BROADBENT, D. E., and GREGORY, M. (1963) 'Vigilance considered as a statistical decision', *Brit. J. Psychol.*, **54**, 309–23.

BROADBENT, D. E., and GREGORY, M. (1964) 'Stimulus set and response set: the alternation of attention', *Quart. J. exp. Psychol.*, **16**, 309–17.

BROADBENT, D. E., and GREGORY, M. (1967) 'Perception of emotionally toned words', *Nature*, **215**, 581–4.

BROADBENT, D. E., and GREGORY, M. (1968) 'Visual perception of words differing in letter diagram frequency', *J. verb. Learn. verb. Behav.*, **7**, 569–71.

BROADBENT, D. E., and GREGORY, M. (1971) 'Effects on tachistoscopic perception from independent variation of word probability and of letter probability', *Acta Psychol.*, **35**, 1–14

BROWN, A. E., and HOPKINS, H. K. (1967) 'Interaction of the auditory and visual sensory modalities', *J. acoust. Soc. Amer.*, **41**, 1–6.

BROWN, C. R., and RUBENSTEIN, H. (1961) 'Test of response bias explanation of word-frequency effect', *Science*, **133**, 280–1.

BROWN, I. D., SIMMONDS, D. C. V., and TICKNER, A. H. (1967) 'Measurement of control skills, vigilance and performance on a subsidiary task during 12-hours car driving', *Ergonomics*, **10**, 665–73.

BROWN, I. D., TICKNER, A. H., and SIMMONDS, D. C. V. (1969) 'Interference between concurrent tasks of driving and telephoning', *J. appl. Psychol.*, **53**, 419–24.

BROWN, R. (1965) *Social Psychology.* New York: The Free Press.

BROWN, R., and FRASER, C. (1963) 'The acquisition of syntax', in C. N. Cofer and B. S. Musgrave (eds.), *Verbal Behavior and Learning*. New York: McGraw-Hill.

BRUNER, J. S. (1957) 'On perceptual readiness', *Psychol. Rev.*, **64**, 123-52.

BRYDEN, M. P. (1964) 'The manipulation of strategies of report in dichotic listening', *Canad. J. Psychol.*, **18**, 126-38.

BUCKNER, D. N., and MCGRATH, J. J. (1963) (eds.) *Vigilance: a Symposium*. New York: McGraw-Hill.

CARR, H. A., and WATSON, J. B. (1908) 'Orientation in the white rat', *J. Comp. Neurol. Psychol.*, **18**, 27-44.

CHOMSKY, N. (1965) *Aspects of the Theory of Syntax*. Cambridge, Mass.: M.I.T. Press.

CHOMSKY, N. (1968) *Language and Mind*. New York: Harcourt, Brace and World, Inc.

CHOMSKY, N. (1971) 'On changing the World', *Cambridge Review*, **92**, 117-36.

CHOMSKY, N., and MILLER, G. A. (1963) 'Introduction to the formal analysis of natural languages', in R. D. Luce, R. R. Bush and E. Galanter (eds.) *Handbook of Mathematical Psychology*, Vol. 2. New York: Wiley.

COCKBURN, A. (1968) 'Introduction', in A. Cockburn and R. Blackburn (eds.), *Student Power*. London: Penguin Books.

CONRAD, R., and HULL, A. J. (1964) 'Information, acoustic confusion, and memory span', *Brit. J. Psychol.*, **55**, 429-32.

CORCORAN, D. W. J. (1966) 'Prediction of responses to multidimensional from responses to unidimensional stimuli', *J. exp. Psychol.*, **71**, 47-54.

CORCORAN, D. W. J., DORFMAN, D. D., and WEENING, D. L. (1968) 'Perceptual independence in speech perception', *Quart. J. exp. Psychol.*, **20**, 336-50.

CORCORAN, D. W. J., and WEENING, D. L. (1969) 'On the combination of evidence from the eye and ear', *Ergonomics*, **12**, 383-94.

DALE, H. C. A. (1966) 'Weighing uncertain evidence: an experiment in probabilistic diagnosis', *Bull. Brit. Psychol. Soc.*, **19**, 3A (Abstract).

EGAN, J. P. (1958) 'Recognition memory and the operating characteristic', *Indiana University Hearing and Communication Lab, Tech Note* AFCRC–TN–58–51.

EMMERICH, D. S., GOLDENBAUM, D. M., HAYDEN, D. L., HOFFMAN, L. S., and TREFFTS, J. L. (1965) 'Meaningfulness as a variable in dichotic hearing', *J. exp. Psychol.*, **69**, 433–6.

EYSENCK, H. J. (1965) *Fact and Fiction in Psychology*. London: Penguin Books.

FODOR, J. A. (1968) *Psychological Explanation*. New York: Random House.

FUCHS, A. H. (1969) 'Recall for order and content of serial word lists in short-term memory', *J. exp. Psychol.*, **82**, 14–21.

GARNER, W. R., and MORTON, J. (1969) 'Perceptual independence: definitions, models and experimental paradigms', *Psychol. Bull.*, **72**, 233–59.

GRAY, J. A., and WEDDERBURN, A. A. I. (1960) 'Grouping strategies with simultaneous stimuli', *Quart. J. exp. Psychol.*, **12**, 180–4.

GWYNNE JONES, H. (1971) 'In search of an idiographic psychology', *Bull. Brit. Psychol. Soc.*, **24**, 279–90.

HABER, R. N. (1966) 'Nature of the effect of set on perception', *Psychol. Rev.*, **73**, 335–51.

HAMMERTON, M. (1962) 'An investigation into the optimal gain of a velocity control system', *Ergonomics*, **5**, 539–43.

HAMMERTON, M. (1963a) 'Transfer of training from a simulated to a real control situation', *J. exp. Psychol.*, **66**, 450–3.

HAMMERTON, M. (1963b) 'Control tasks with extended distances between operation and display', *Ergonomics*, **6**, 413–18.

HAMMERTON, M. (1964a) 'The components of acquisition time', *Ergonomics*, **7**, 91–3.

HAMMERTON, M., and TICKNER, A. H. (1964b) 'Transfer of training between space oriented and body oriented control situations', *Brit. J. Psychol.*, **55**, 433–7.

HOCKEY, G. R. J. (1970) 'Signal probability and spatial location as possible bases for increased selectivity in noise', *Quart. J. exp. Psychol.*, **22**, 37–42.

HOLLOWAY, C. M. (1970) 'Consonant recognition with two levels of decision complexity', *Quart. J. exp. Psychol.*, **22**, 467–74.

HUDSON, L. (1966) *Contrary Imaginations*. London: Methuen.

HUDSON, L. (1970) 'The choice of Hercules', *Bull. Brit. Psychol. Soc.* **23**, 287–92.

INGLEBY, J. D. (1969) Decision-making processes in human perception and memory. Ph.D. Thesis, University of Cambridge.

INGLEBY, J. D. (1970) 'Ideology and the human sciences'. *The Human Context*, **2**, 159–87.

JACKSON, W. (Chairman) (1966) *Report on the 1965 Triennial Manpower Survey of Engineers, Technologists, Scientists and Technical Supporting Staff*. Cmnd. 3103. London: H.M.S.O.

JAKOBOVITS, L. A., and LAMBERT, W. E. (1962) 'Mediated satiation in verbal transfer', *J. exp. Psychol.*, **64**, 346–51.

JAMES, W. (1890) *Principles of Psychology*. New York: Henry Holt.

JOYNSON, R. B. (1970) 'The breakdown of modern psychology', *Bull. Brit. Psychol. Soc.*, **23**, 261–70.

LAING, R. D. (1967) *The Politics of Experience*. London: Penguin Books.

LAMING, D. R. J. (1968) *Information Theory of Choice-Reaction Times*. London: Academic Press.

LAWRENCE, D. H., and COLES, G. R. (1954) 'Accuracy of recognition with alternatives before and after the stimulus', *J. exp. Psychol.*, **47**, 208–14.

LIBERMAN, A. M., COOPER, F. S., HARRIS, K. S., AND MACNEILAGE, P. F. (1963) 'Motor theory of speech perception' (Abstract *J. acoust. Soc. Amer.*, **35**, 1114). Proc. Speech Communication Seminar, Stockholm.

LIGHT, L. L., and CARTER-SOBELL, L. (1970) 'Effect of changed semantic context on recognition memory', *J. verb. Learn. verb Behav.*, **9**, 1–11.

LINDSAY, R. K., and LINDSAY, J. M. (1966) 'Reaction time and serial versus parallel information processing', *J. exp. Psychol.*, **71**, 294–303.

LOVELESS, N. E. (1957) *Air Ministry Flying Personnel Research Committee Report No. 1027*.

LURIA, A. R. (1961) *The role of speech in the regulation of normal and abnormal behaviour*. London: Pergamon.

MACINTYRE, A. (1970) *Marcuse*. London: Fontana.

MACKINTOSH, N. J. (1962) 'The effects of overtraining on a reversal and a non-reversal shift', *J. comp. physiol. Psychol.*, **55**, 555–9.

MACKINTOSH, N. J. (1965) 'Overtraining, transfer to proprioceptive control, and position reversal', *Quart. J. exp. Psychol.*, **17**, 26–36.

MARPLES, D. L. (1960) 'The decisions of engineering design', *Engng. Desr.*, December.

MCLEOD, P., WILLIAMS, C. E., and BROADBENT, D. E. (1971) 'Free recall with assistance from one and from two retrieval cues', *Brit. J. Psychol.*, **62**, 59–65.

MEDAWAR, P. (1969) 'On the effecting of all things possible', *New Scientist*, **43**, 465–7.

MEHLER, J. (1963) 'Some effects of grammatical transformations on the recall of English sentences', *J. verb. Learn. verb. Behav.*, **2**, 346–51.

MILLER, G. A. (1969) 'Psychology as a means of promoting human welfare', *Amer. Psychol.*, **24**, 1063–75.

MILLER, G. A., GALANTER, E., and PRIBRAM, K. H. (1960) *Plans and the structure of Behavior*. New York: Henry Holt.

MORAY, N. (1960) 'Broadbent's filter theory: Postulate H and the problem of switching time', *Quart. J. exp. Psychol.*, **12**, 214–20.

MORAY, N. (1961) 'Perceptual defence and filter theory', *Nature*, **191**, 940.

MORTON, J. (1969a) 'Interaction of information in word recognition', *Psychol. Rev.*, **76**, 165–78.

MORTON, J. (1969b) 'What could possibly be innate?', Proc. Int. Cong. Appl. Linguistics.

MOYNIHAN, D. P. (1970) 'The role of the social scientist in action research', *Social Science Research Council Newsletter*, November, 2–5.

NATIONAL SCIENCE FOUNDATION. (1960) *American Science Manpower 1960* N.S.F. 62–43. Washington: U.S. Government Printing Office.

NEISSER, U. (1963) 'The multiplicity of thought', *Brit. J. Psychol.*, **54**, 1–14.

NEISSER, U. (1967) *Cognitive Psychology*. New York: Appleton Century Crofts.

NEWELL, A., SHAW, J. C., and SIMON, H. A. (1958) 'Elements of a theory of human problem solving', *Psychol. Rev.*, **65**, 151–66.

NEWELL, A., and SIMON, H. A. (1959) *The Simulation of Human Thought*. Rand Corporation Paper P-1734 Santa Monica: California.

NEWELL, A., and SIMON, H. A. (1972) *Human Problem Solving*. New York: Prentice-Hall.

NEWSWEEK. (1967) Vol. **69**, No. 12, p. 48.

NOBLE, M., FITTS, P. M., and WARREN, C. E. (1955) 'The frequency response of skilled subjects in a pursuit tracking task', *J. exp. Psychol.*, **49**, 249–56.

NOTT, K. (1969) 'The unnatural history of human aggression', *Encounter*, **33**, Part V, November.

OLDFIELD, R. C., and WINGFIELD, A. (1964) 'The time it takes to name an object', *Nature*, **202**, 1031–2.

OSGOOD, C. E., SUCI, G. J., and TANNENBAUM, P. H. (1957) *The Measurement of Meaning*. Urbana: University of Illinois Press.

PASK, G. (1971) *Learning Strategies and Individual Competence*, Report on SSRC Grant HR 983/1: System Research Ltd.

PHILLIPS, L., and EDWARDS, W. (1966) 'Conservatism in a simple probability inference task', *J. exp. Psychol.*, **72**, 346–54.

POLLACK, I. (1964) 'Interaction of two sources of verbal context in word identification', *Lang. Speech*, **7**, 1–12.

R. (1969) 'Column', *Encounter*, **33**, Part II, August, 42–4.

RABBITT, P. M. A. (1964) 'Ignoring irrelevant information', *Brit. J. Psychol.*, **55**, 403–14.

RABBITT, P. M. A. (1966) 'Identification of some stimuli embedded among others', *Proc. XVIII Intern. Cong. Psychol.* Moscow. Symposium 17.

RESTLE, F. (1961) *Psychology of Judgment and Choice*. New York: Wiley.

ROLFE, J. M. (1969) 'Human factors and the display of height information', *Applied Ergonomics*, **1**, 16–24.

SANFORD, A. J. (1969) Experiments on simple reaction time in relation to loudness. Ph.D. Thesis, University of Cambridge.

SANFORD, A. J. (1971) 'Effects of changes in the intensity of white noise on simultaneity judgments and simple reaction time', *Quart. J. exp. Psychol.*, **23**, 296–303.

SCHON, D. A. (1971) *Beyond the Stable State*. London: Maurice Temple Smith.

SHAW, B. W. (1970) 'Religion and conceptual models of behaviour', *Brit. J. soc. clin. Psychol.*, **9**, 320–7.

SHOTTER, J. (1970) 'The philosophy of psychology', *Bull. Brit. Psychol. Soc.*, **80**, 207–12.

SKINNER, B. F. (1957) *Verbal Behaviour*. London: Methuen.

SUTHERLAND, N. S., MACKINTOSH, N. J., and WOLFE, J. B. (1965) 'Extinction as a function of the order of partial and consistent reinforcement', *J. exp. Psychol.*, **69**, 56–59.

SWETS, J. A. (ed.) (1964) *Signal Detection and Recognition by Human Observers*. New York: Wiley.

TANNENBAUM, P. H., and WILLIAMS, F. (1968) 'Prompted word replacement in active and passive sentences', *Lang. Speech*, **11**, 220–9.

THOMAS, O. (1965) *Transformational Grammar and the Teacher of English*. New York: Holt, Rinehart and Winston.

TORREY, J. (1969) 'The learning of grammatical patterns', *J. verb. Learn. verb. Behav.*, **8**, 360–8.

TREISMAN, A. M. (1960) 'Contextual cues in selective listening', *Quart. J. exp. Psychol.*, **12**, 242–8.

TRUMBO, D., and NOBLE, M. (1970) 'Secondary task effects on serial verbal learning', *J. exp. Psychol.*, **85**, 418–24.

TULVING, E., MANDLER, G., and BAUMAL, R. (1964) 'Interaction of two sources of information in tachistoscopic word recognition', *Canad. J. Psychol.*, **18**, 62–71.

TULVING, E., and OSLER, S. (1968) 'Effectiveness of retrieval cues in memory for words', *J. exp. Psychol.*, **77**, 593–601.

VENABLES, P. H. (1964) 'Performance and level of activation in schizophrenics and normals', *Brit. J. Psychol.*, **55**, 207–18.

VICKERY, B. C. (1965) *On Retrieval System Theory*. London: Butterworth. (2nd ed.)

WARNOCK, M. (1965) *The Philosophy of Sartre*. London: Hutchinson.

WARR, P. B., and KNAPPER, C. (1968) *The Perception of People and Events*. London: Wiley.

WICKELGREN, W. A. (1965) 'Acoustic similarity and intrusion errors in short-term memory', *J. exp. Psychol.*, **70**, 102–8.

WRIGHT, P. (1969) 'Transformations and the understanding of sentences', *Lang. Speech*, **12**, 156–66.

YNTEMA, D. B., and TRASK, F. P. (1963) 'Recall as a search process', *J. verb. Learn. verb. Behav.*, **2**, 65–74.

Index

Acoustic similarity, 156–7, 158
Agnew, Spiro, 61
Anisfeld, M., 72
Attitudes, prediction of, 41–4
Audley, R. J., 21, 22

Baddeley, A. D., 160
Bahrick, H. P., 193
Baumal, R., 52
Bayesian approach, 11, 32–3, 34, 38
  in combination of evidence, 47, 50–63
  in retrieval from memory, 86
Behaviourism, 5, 8, 103, 124, 127, 188, 189
Behaviour therapy, 127–8
Bold, Alan, 103
Boring, Professor, 83
Bousfield, W. A., 149
Braine, M. D. S., 203
Briggs, G. E., 193
Brill, A. A., 127
Broadbent, D. E., 22, 34, 35, 36, 56, 69, 73, 76, 84, 85, 86, 89, 99, 115, 137, 139, 140, 147, 148, 150, 152, 165, 173, 176, 179
Brown, A. E., 176
Brown, C. R., 140
Brown, I. D., 30
Brown, R., 44, 204
Bruner, J. S., 127
Bryden, M. P., 148
Buckner, D. N., 47, 176

Campbell, John W., 8

Carr, H. A., 19
Carroll, Lewis, 155
Carter-Sobell, L., 90
Chomsky, N., 8, 10, 42, 189, 191, 195–8, 208, 209
Cockburn, A., 189
Cohen, B. H., 149
Coles, G. R., 106
Command signal, 18–22, 28, 109
Computer function:
  analogy with control of behaviour, 125–6, 128–30
  analogy with human language, 130–2, 153–4
  in problem solving, 18, 171
  software, 107–8, 129–30
Conrad, R., 156
Control of behaviour:
  external, 10
  internal, 109–10, 125–9
Control of movement, 13–16
Cooper, F. S., 139
Corcoran, D. W. J., 45, 47, 177
Cromwell, Oliver, 43, 63, 119
Crosland, Anthony, 42
Cultural differences, 6–8, 41–2, 83, 163–4, 182–5

Dale, H. C. A., 160, 174
Decision-making (*see also* Evidence), 23–31, 37–8, 169–80
  serial processing, 174–8
  simultaneous processing, 178–80
  successive stages in, 27–30
Descartes, 117

Dewey Decimal System, *see* Retrieval systems
Dorfman, D. D., 45

Edwards, Ward, 61, 174
Egan, J. P., 54
Eliot, George, 143
Eliot, T. S., 111, 116, 120
Emmerich, D. S., 148
Empirical method, 8, 38, 64, 208
  in psychology, 187–9, 205–7
L'Être et Le Néant, 119
Evidence:
  accumulation of, 23–8, 30, 40, 109
  Bayesian model, 50–63
  combination of, 44–64, 174–7
  linear model, 45–6, 49–50
Eysenck, H. J., 128
Existential thought, 8, 66, 119–20

Fascism, 89, 119–20
Fitts, P. M., 193
Fodor, J. A., 5, 101
Fraser, C., 204
Freedom, 10, 108, 112, 117–20
Freud, Anna, 83
Friedman, Milton, 61
Fuchs, A. H., 95

Galanter, E., 17, 18
Garner, W. R., 44
Giddings, 90
Giotto, 192
Goals, 17–18
Godden, Duncan, 61
Goldenbaum, D. M., 148
Grammar:
  context sensitive rules, 198, 201
  grammaticality, 194–7, 208
  rewriting rules, 17, 167, 190, 197–8, 201
  transformational rules, 168–9, 190–8, 200
  use of pronouns, 195–7
Gray, J. A., 148
Gregory, M., 35, 36, 69, 73, 148, 150, 152, 173, 176

Gwynne Jones, H., 111

Haber, R. N., 105, 106
Hammerton, M., 15, 16, 19
Harris, K. S., 139
Harvard University, 67, 72, 116, 127
Hayden, D. L., 148
Hitch, Graham, 95, 96
Hockey, G. R. J., 77
Hoffman, L. S., 148
Holloway, C. M., 36, 46
Hopkins, H. K., 176
Hudson, L., 8, 115
Hull, A. J., 156
Hull, Clark, 20

Ingleby, J. D., 8, 56
Instrument design, 4–5

Jackson, W., 163
Jakobovits, L. A., 127
James, W., 20–2
Johnson, Paul, 155
Joynson, R. B., 7

Knapper, C., 63

Laing, R. D., 10, 111
Lambert, W. E., 127
Laming, D. R. J., 22
Language (*see also* Grammar, Word association and Word perception):
  acquisition, 17, 166–7, 191, 202–5
  linguistic competence and performance, 193–4, 208
  noun phrase as an address, 131–6, 153–5, 161
Lawrence, D. H, 106
Learning:
  in animals, 19, 126, 201–2
  language, *see* Language acquisition
Liberman, A. M., 139
Light, L. L., 90
Limitations of nervous system, 11, 23, 46–7
Lindsay, J. M., 179
Lindsay, R. K., 179

Loveless, N. E., 176
Luria, A. R., 127

MacIntyre, A., 43
Mackintosh, N. J., 126
MacNeilage, P. F., 139
Mandler, G., 52
Marples, D. L., 170
McGrath, J. J., 47, 176
McLeod, P., 85, 86, 89, 99
Medawar, P., 43
Mehler, J., 168
Memory:
    analogy with computers, 153
    filing systems, 83-4, 86, 96-8, 143,
        157-9
    libraries, 97-9, 145-7, 150, 159-60
    components of, 86-8
    long-term, 86-7, 161
    recognition, 90-4
    retrieval, 84-6, 89-91, 95-6, 146,
        149-52, 156-9
    short-term, 87, 156, 160
    use of addresses, 88, 131-5
Michelangelo, 192, 193
Middlemarch, see Eliot, George
Miller, G. A., 8, 17, 18, 198
Moray, N., 137, 152
Morton, J., 44, 52, 205
Moynihan, D. P., 8
Myers, C. S., 188

National Science Foundation, 163
Nazis, 119-20
Neisser, U., 104, 178, 179
Newell, A., 18, 171, 179, 180
Newsweek, 6, 172
Nixon, President, 60
Noble, M., 30, 193
Noise, behavioural effects of, 76-7
Nott, K., 188

Oldfield, R. C., 135
Osgood, C. E., 182
Osler, S., 85, 89

Pask, G., 113

Perception, theories of, 33-7
Perceptual defence, 67, 69-80, 136
Perceptual selection (*see also* Word
    perception), 105-6, 109, 115,
    136-7, 147-50
Phillips, L., 174
Pike, A. R., 22
Pollack, I., 52
Positivism, 32, 67
Pribram, K. H., 17, 18
Problem solving, 169-72
Psychiatry, 10, 111, 112

R., 189
Rabbitt, P. M. A., 178
Reaction studies, 22-9
Reid, Ian, 183
Repression, 67
Response interference, 105
Restle, F., 173, 183
Retrieval systems (*see also* Memory),
    112-13, 159-60
    Dewey Decimal, 97, 99, 145, 159
The Roads to Freedom, 119
Rolfe, J. M., 4
Royal Society, The, 44, 117
Rubenstein, H., 140
Russell, Lord, 42, 194

Sanford, A. J., 29
Sartre, Jean-Paul, 10, 117, 119
Schon, D. A., 8
Scientific manpower, allocation of,
    163-4
Scientific method, 31-3
Semantic differential, 181-5
Shakespeare, 66
Shaw, B. W., 41
Shaw, J. C., 18, 171, 179, 180
Shotter, J., 8
Simmonds, D. C. V., 30
Simon, H. A., 18, 171, 179, 180
Simulators, 13-14
Skinner, B. F., 125
Socialism, 42
Sofer, Cyril, 188

Strategies in mental performance, 12, 104–6
  filtering, 115
  holist-serialist comparison, 113–15
  pigeon-holing, 115
Suci, G. J., 182
Sutherland, N. S., 126
Swets, J. A., 141, 176

Tannenbaum, P. H., 182, 199, 200
Teaching-machine programs, 114
Thomas, O., 167, 194
Tickner, A. H., 19, 30
Torrey, J., 203
Trask, F. P., 147–51
Travers, Bob., 183
Treffts, J. L., 148
Treisman, A. M., 137
Trumbo, D., 30
Tulving, E., 52, 85, 89

Venables, P. H., 124
Vickery, B. C., 159
Visual search, 104, 178–9

Warnock, M., 65
Warr, P. B., 63
Warren, C. E., 193
Watson, J. B., 19
Wedderburn, A. A. I., 111
Weening, D. L., 45, 47
Wickelgren, W. A., 156
Williams, C. E., 85, 86, 89, 99
Williams, F., 199, 200
Winchester College, 41–2
Wingfield, A., 135
Wingrove, Miss, 90
Wolfe, J. B., 126
Word association, 123, 161
Word perception, 35–6, 52
  common and uncommon words, 53–5, 68, 138–41
  emotional words, *see* perceptual defence
  funnel vision in, 77–9
Wright, P., 188, 199, 200

Yntema, D. B., 147–51

POINT LOMA COLLEGE

RYAN LIBRARY